William Huntington

A Rule And A Riddle

Or, An Everlasting Task For Blind Watchmen And Old Women

William Huntington

A Rule And A Riddle

Or, An Everlasting Task For Blind Watchmen And Old Women

ISBN/EAN: 9783337115937

Printed in Europe, USA, Canada, Australia, Japan

Cover: Foto ©ninafisch / pixelio.de

More available books at **www.hansebooks.com**

A RULE AND A RIDDLE;

OR,

AN EVERLASTING TASK

FOR

BLIND WATCHMEN AND OLD WOMEN.

IN A LETTER TO A FRIEND.

By WILLIAM HUNTINGTON, S. S.

MINISTER OF THE GOSPEL

AT PROVIDENCE CHAPEL, LITTLE TITCHFIELD-STREET; AND AT MONKWELL STREET CHAPEL, IN THE CITY.

Forasmuch as we have heard, that certain which went out from us have troubled you with words, subverting your souls, saying, Ye must be circumcised, and keep the law; to whom we gave no such commandment. It seemeth good to the Holy Ghost, and to us, to lay upon you no greater burden than these necessary things; that ye abstain from meats offered to idols, and from blood, and from things strangled, and from fornication: from which, if ye keep yourselves, ye shall do well. Fare ye well. Which when they had read, they rejoiced for the consolation.

Acts xv. 24. 28, 29. 31.

LONDON:

PRINTED BY T. BENSLEY;

And sold by G. Terry, Paternoster-row; J. Chalmers, No. 210, Whitecross-street, near Moorfields; J. Davidson, No. 7, Postern-row, Tower-hill; Mr. Baker, No. 226, Oxford-street; Mrs. Howes, No. 15, Charles-street; at Monkwell-street Chapel every Tuesday evening; at Providence Chapel, Titchfield-street; by Mr. Mantle, Lewes, Sussex; Mr. Fenley, Broad Mead, Bristol; and by Mr. Chamberlain, Portsmouth.

M, DC C, LXXXVIII.

PREFACE.

CHRISTIAN READER,

I BEGAN the following letter with an intent to send it as an answer to a very polite one sent by an unknown friend to me: it came without a name, but I was to direct it to him with the initials of his name to a certain number. When I had written about thirty folio pages of manuscript, I felt an inclination rising in my mind to publish it; and as the gentleman informs me that he sometimes hears me, I thought it was sure to fall into his hands: and as he seems to be an earnest inquirer after truth, I see no cause why he should be offended at the publication of it, as I think it is an answer of truth, and seeing it may be useful to other inquirers as well as to him, if God's blessing should attend it.

I wish thee, Reader, to lay by all prejudice, and to settle *thy faith in no man's wisdom*, but *in the power of God*; and to do by this letter as God does with Zion—*he lays judgment to the line, and righteousness*

righteousness to the plummet,—and sweeps away all refuges of lies, and deluges all the hiding places of hypocrites. And if thou wilt *come to the light*, if thou desirest to be *found in the faith*, then criticise and scrutinize this little piece over and over again, and lay it to the word of God, and try it soundly by that standard, and see whether this be *Antinomianism*, or whether it be *the everlasting gospel of Jesus Christ*, and judge accordingly. And when thou hast satisfied thyself on that head—then compare it with the tracts of those evangelists who make *the killing letter* the *rule of life*; and when thou hast compared these together, and tried both by the word of God, then let the name of *Antinomian* be saddled upon the right ass. Give not up the *good old way*, though, according to prophecy, the *way of truth be evil spoken of*; but *set thine heart to the high-way*, and *turn not to the right hand, nor to the left*, but run the race set before thee, *looking to Jesus the author and finisher of faith*.

And when thou hearest men in a pulpit begin to cut at others as Antinomians, without describing what they are, and dropping the subject of the gospel, saying, "but we must do justice to the law, for it is the believer's only rule of life;" then watch their countenance, and observe the Scripture proofs that they bring; and if their *countenance falls*, their tongue gets *fettered*, and no proof produced but a jumble of confusion, let it convince

convince thee that they have not *stood in God's council*—therefore he has *confounded them before thee*; Wisdom is justified *of her children*, and her *children are to stir up themselves against the hypocrite*.

The Scriptures tell thee that the man who hath *not the doctrine of Christ hath not God*; and that those who bring not *Christ's doctrine are not to be received:* And by the doctrine and spirit of Christ the *children of God* and the *children of the devil are made manifest.* But in our days matters are altered; the pure gospel is called *Antinomianism: valour* for truth, *zeal* for God, *fervour* in devotion, and *earnestness* in preaching, are called the " effects of a bad spirit?" But, twisting like the serpent, warping like the willow, shaping a conversation and a sermon to *please all* and offend none, except it be the experimental Christian;—these are the effects or fruits of an *excellent spirit,*—this is the *quintessence* of *candour*; this is *doing the work of an evangelist,* and *making full proof of the ministry.* These people will not be thy judges, Reader, in the great day; Christ is thy judge,—and it is not what is called candour, that will acquit thee at his bar; it is the *word* and *Spirit* of *truth* that must make *thee free, if thou wilt be free indeed;* the *word that I have spoken,* says Christ, *the same shall judge them in the great day.*

Be not offended, Reader, at the title of this little piece,—*A Rule and a Riddle*; or, *An Ever-*

lasting Task for Blind Watchmen and Old Women. It is taken from real facts,—from a synod that was convened, consisting of some *watchmen* and some *old women*; where counsel was taken against *one* that never took counsel against them. I call it an everlasting task, because I think the doctrines cannot be overthrown. It is not directed to any body; if every body be innocent, it can be applicable to none; no person has a right to make application unless he be concerned. The *Rule* and the *Riddle* both, with respect to application, are to those to whom they may belong, and for the use, information, or satisfaction of any that chuse to try their skill. Reader, fare thee well, and forget not that it is by the testimony of God's word, of his Spirit, and of thy own conscience, that thou must stand or fall at the bar of God;— therefore, love the truth and peace; while I rest and remain (with the little knowledge that God has been pleased to give me) thy servant in the truth, and for the truth's sake,

WILLIAM HUNTINGTON, S. S.

RULE AND A RIDDLE, &c.

DEAR SIR,

I RECEIVED the packet which you directed to me, confisting of your *very long epistle*, of a *circular letter in print*, and of a *sermon on the promises of God*. I read your epistle without offence, as I believe you meant well, which I gather from your polite address, civil treatment, and cautious way of expressing yourself; such a letter I have never received from any person who has thought proper to *expose* or *oppose* me, as a maintainer of licentious doctrines. Their letters have generally been filled with the scurrility of Billingsgate, and without any truth fairly stated—which has only served ferved to convince me that such persons *are without Christ, and have no hope in the world.*

Was it in my power, I would addrefs you as a *Gentleman of sense* and *a scholar,* for both appear in your affectionate epistle; but I have neither politeness nor learning, as it is now called, yet will give you the best answer I am capable of, in the language of Scripture.

If I know any thing of my own heart, I can truly assert—that I wish *all that fear God to know what he hath done for my soul;* and, in declaring it, I desire *to speak as the oracles of God*; and to live up to what I preach, as far as grace shall enable me while in this body of death; and I wish some of our zealous *advocates for Moses* would do the same, by letting *their light shine before men,* that others *might see* as well as *hear* of *their good works*; seeing it is *not the hearers* nor the contenders for *the law that are just before God;—but the doers of the law shall be justified.*

That the ten commandments are the believer's only *rule of life,* was insisted upon by the first person that I ever disputed with on that subject; which he endeavoured to enforce and prove by Paul's quoting part of it in his *Epistle to the Romans,* which church he supposed to confift of saints only—by Paul's addressing them as the *beloved of God called to be saints.* Not considering that *lilies and thorns, servants and sons, Israelites and hypocrites,*

hypocrites, wife virgins and foolish ones, are to go and *grow together as tares and wheat until harvest*. And on the account of this mixture it is that the *killing letter* and the *promise of life* must go together; the promises are to the *heirs of promise* ; and we know that what *things soever the law saith, it saith to them who are under the law*, Rom. iii. 19. I asked the Gentleman which of the commandments he meant? And he replied, " Those in the 20th chapter of Exodus." And if those ten commandments are *the believer's only rule* —the other parts of Scripture one would think might be dispensed with by the believer; for, if that law be his only rule of life, what can he want more? Though, by the by, there is not the command *to love God* in that chapter.

" If the ten commandments in the letter be the believer's only rule," *Abel, who obtained witness that he was righteous, God testifying of his gifts*, had no rule to go by. *Enoch walked with God three hundred years*, Gen. v. 22. and was *translated that he should not see death*; for *before his translation he had this testimony, that he pleased God*, Heb. xi. 5. yet had no rule of life. *Noah the just*, who took the *warning of God, prepared an ark, condemned the world, and became heir of an everlasting righteousness*, was without rule. *Abraham, the friend of God*, and the *father of the faithful*, and *heir of the world*, must walk at an uncertainty also. *Melchisedec, king of righteousness,*

righteousness, and *king of peace*, *priest of the Most High God*—after whose order Christ is a priest for ever and ever,—had NO RULE for his ORDER. Yea, all the *anti-deluvian* and *post-deluvian saints*, down to the time of the children of Israel's compassing the Mount Sinai, must be left to walk and to worship at random; for, if the *letter of the law*, or the *ten commandments delivered at Sinai*, be the believer's *only rule of life*, it is clear they were *without that rule*. Yet they *were not without law to God*, for they *feared him*, *loved him*, and *walked with him*,—and they were under the *law of faith to Christ*—*for they saw* [him] *at a distance and embraced him*, were *united to him*, and became *one spirit with him*.

I have sometimes wondered why these antient saints should be set forth with the encomiums of being *God's friends*, *walking with him*, *obtaining witness* that they were *righteous*, *obtaining promises*, obtaining *good report*, as strangers and *pilgrims upon earth*, of *whom the world was not worthy*, *seeking an heavenly country*, and a *city that hath foundations*, despising all worldly pleasure, pelf, and honour, leaving their *own house*, home, and country, without any *desire to return thither*; and why we should be commanded to *go forth by the footsteps of this flock*, and be said to be *compassed about with this cloud of witnesses*, and be directed to follow those *who through faith and patience now inherit the promises*;—

when

when we know that if they were on earth, in this refined age, they would be ranked among the worst of Antinomians.

It is strange that the believer is not commanded to look to *Moses the lawgiver*, and *to the bondwoman that is under the law*, instead of *looking to Abraham our father, and to Sarah that bare us, whom God called alone, and blessed and increased*, Isaiah li. 2. Paul would have us *tread in the steps of the faith of our father Abraham, which he had being yet uncircumcised*, and declares that *the promise that he should be the heir of the world, was not to him, or to his seed, through the law*, Rom. iv. 12, 13. and yet affirms, that as *many as are of faith are blessed with faithful Abraham*.—And this promised *blessing*, and promised *heirship*, was given to *Abraham*, and to his *seed—four hundred and thirty years before the law*, or before our *only rule of life* was given.

What *rule* had those glorious *pilgrims* to walk by, who *obtained so good a report*, or *so good* a (testimony) from God?—Paul tells us, that *Abel offered* to God, and *obtained witness that he was righteous* BY FAITH—then *faith was his rule of worship:—* that *Enoch walked with God* BY FAITH—then faith was his *rule of walk:* that Noah *condemned the world by faith*—then *faith was his rule of judgment*. *By faith Abraham, when he was called, went out not knowing whither he went*—then faith was his *rule*, by which he took his journey, though he knew not whither,

whither, and his obedience was the obedience of faith. But if he had been favoured with our *only rule of life,* he might have known whither he was going, and not have gone in ignorance, and his obedience would have been the obedience of the law instead of faith.—But Paul will have it that all Abraham's children are in the same strait that their father was—*for they walk by faith, not by sight.*—But if the letter of the law be the *only rule* that the believer is to walk and live by, then he *walks by sight* not *by faith ;* he *looks at the things that are seen, not at the things which are not seen.*—It is by *faith that Moses saw him who is invisible,* and *by faith we must look at the things that are not seen, which are eternal.*

Paul says, that he that cometh to God *must believe that he is, and that he is a rewarder of them that diligently seek him ;* then *faith* must be the *rule* of his coming. We have *access by faith into this grace wherein we stand,* Rom. v. 2.—then *faith* is the *rule* of our *approach* to God. The *just* [man] *shall live by his faith,* Hab. ii. 4.—then *faith* is the just man's *rule of life.* We *walk by faith, not by sight,* 2 Cor. v. 7.—then *faith* is our *rule of walk.* Thou *standest by faith,* says Paul, Rom. xi. 20.—then *faith* is the *rule* of the believer's standing. Whatever ye shall *ask believing, ye shall receive,* says Christ ;—then *faith is the rule* of that branch of worship. By *faith Enoch had this testimony, that he pleased God;* but
without

without faith it is impossible to please him, Heb. xi. 5, 6.—then faith is a *rule* that God approves of, and is pleased with. *Whatsoever is not of faith is sin*—then *faith* is a *perfect rule of holiness*. He *that believes is justified from all things, from which he could not by the law of Moses*—then *faith* is our *rule of righteousness*. It is by *faith that we overcome the world*. To *lay hold on eternal life, is to fight the good fight of faith*, according to Paul; *I have fought a good fight, I have finished my course, I have kept the faith*—then faith was the *rule* of his *warfare*, and the *rule* of his *race*; and it was the grace of God that made Paul obedient to that rule. *We have received grace and apostleship for obedience to the faith*, Rom. i. 5. that is, *by Christ we have received grace* to save our souls, *and apostleship* to be of use to the church, not as a reward of our obedience, but to furnish us with power to make us *obedient to the faith, among all nations for his name*, Rom. i. 5.—then faith is the *rule* of apostolic *obedience*; for it cannot be called receiving grace for *obedience to the faith*, if *faith* be not the gracious man's *rule* of obedience.

Paul counts *all things but dung that he may win Christ, and be found in him; not having his own righteousness, which is of the law, but that which is through the faith of Christ*; and tells us to *walk by the same rule, and mind the same thing*, Phil. iii. If you take this *rule* of Paul's to be his *pressing forward*, or any of *his attainments*, it is answered, by *faith* he
pressed

pressed forward, and by *faith he attained*; for else his *pressing* and *attaining* had been nothing but sin; for *whatsoever is not of faith*, according to Paul's doctrine, is *sin*.

By faith *Christ dwells in our hearts*, and by *faith we dwell in him*; and in *Christ Jesus neither circumcision availeth any thing, nor uncircumcision, but a new creature*, which is *Christ formed within us:* and *as many as walk according to this* RULE, *peace be on them and mercy, and upon the Israel of God*, Gal. vi. 15, 16. *Faith* is the *rule* of *life* according to the revealed will of God in Christ Jesus; *and this is the* WILL *of him that sent me, that every one which seeth the Son, and* BELIEVETH *on him, may have everlasting life, and I will raise him up at the last day,* John vi. 40. Thus *faith* appears to be the *believer's rule of life*, according to the will of God in Christ Jesus; and the *letter of the law* is the *bond-children's rule of life*—he that *doth these things shall live in them*. Let him *do* according to this *rule* and he shall live. The law is not the *rule* of *believing* but of *doing*; the *law is not of faith* but of works, and *the man that doth them shall live in them*, Gal. iii. 12.

If to *see the Son*, and *believe on him*, entitles us to *everlasting life* according to God's will, then *faith* must be the *rule* of that *life*; and one would think that, if *he that liveth and believeth shall never die, faith* must be a safe *rule* to *live* by.

I have

I have sometimes thought that, if the letter of the law in the 20th chapter of Exodus be the believer's only rule of life, he would be sorely put to his shifts when the devil sets a troop of *Arians, Socinians* or *Sabellians* at him; he would find these words—*I am the Lord thy God, which have brought thee out of the land of Egypt, and out of the house of bondage; thou shalt have no other gods before me.* This *rule* would hardly set him right. It is by *faith* that we *apprehend Christ*; it is by faith we *lay hold* of *him*, as the hope set before us, Heb. vi. 18. It is *by* Christ *that we believe in God*, 1 Pet. i. 21. and we *receive the promise of the Spirit through faith*, Gal. iii. 14. By this *rule* we come to a saving knowledge of the Trinity; for the eye of faith is a light by which we see *what is the fellowship of the mystery*, Eph. iii. 9. Without *the* ASSURANCE *of understanding, there will be no true acknowledgment of the mystery of God* [the Holy Ghost], *and of the Father and of Christ*, Col. ii. 2. The ten commandments will never guide a man into this mystery, nor set him right if he errs in it.

In your epistle, Sir, you tell me that, " if I do not enforce the law as the believer's rule of life, I must in some sense make it void." I think I have sufficiently proved that Paul's *rule of life* and *walk* was *faith*; and he asks, *Do we then make void the law through faith? God forbid; yea, we establish the*

the law, Rom. iii. 31. Paul infifts upon it that faith *worketh by love*, and tells us that *love worketh no ill to his neighbour*; therefore *love is the fulfilling of the law*, Rom. xiii. 10. If this doctrine be *the fulfilling of the law*, it *cannot make it void*.

The fermon that you was fo kind as to fend me is pregnant with a deal of fcholaftic unfcriptural logic, little better than nonfenfe, which may ferve to difplay the worldly wifdom of the author, and excite the admiration of unenlightened people. But any fpiritual perfon will eafily perceive that he knows little or nothing of the *killing letter of the law*, or of the *fpiritual power* of the gofpel.

The law, as the believer's *rule of life*, he endeavours to enforce " from the fitnefs of things," which are phrafes that ftand for any thing or nothing, juft as the author pleafes. But he does not fatisfy me concerning the *things* that *fit*. God grant he may not go out of the world with this confufion in his heart! if he does it is to be feared that he will find the *miniftration of death*—and his *carnal mind*—when they come to gripe one another in a dying hour, will not *fit* fo eafy as he imagines. Paul *delighted in the law of God after the inward man*, Rom. vii. 22. And, according to Paul, the *law of God* and the *inward man* are things that will fit; *a new heart* and a *new fpirit* are things that *join* well; a fenfe of *God's love* to us, and a *pure love* to him, brings about an union that fits fweetly.

sweetly. *Believe,* says the Saviour, *that I am in you and you in me:* and when *Christ crucified* and a *broken heart* come together, they are *things* that *fit* as exactly as the *branch in the vine,* or as the foundation with the superstructure.—And if the author of this sermon dies a stranger to " the *fitness of these things,"* as he seems to be at present, it had been good for him if he had never been born. Persons who are strangers to an union with Christ by the Spirit know nothing savingly of the spiritual *fitness of things;* they may make a noise about the law just to blind folks, but they bring forth no more fruit to God's glory than a *branch* that is *not in the vine,* John xv. 4.

A friend of mine once asked a certain divine in London " What he thought of the law as the *believer's only rule of life?"* He replied " The believer must look with one eye to Christ, and with the other to the law." But he brought no more proof from the word of God than this author has, who attempts to prove it by the *fitness of things.* My friend replied " Then every believer must squint." However, there is no call for squinting in this matter; Christ says, *Look unto me, and be saved, all ye ends of the earth;* and adds, *I will keep that man in perfect peace whose mind is stayed on me:* and Paul tells us to *run the race set before us looking to Jesus, the author and finisher of our faith,* Heb. xii. 2. " Looking with one eye to the law, and with the other to Chrift," is erring from wifdom's rule of direction; which is, *Let thine eyes look right on, and let thine eyelids look ftraight before thee.—Ponder the path of thy feet, and let all thy ways be eftablifhed,* Prov. iv. 25, 26.

The *printed letter* that you fent me is a *difcord* upon the fame ftring I perceive; but the author will never be able to prove from the Scriptures of truth, that the *ten commandments in the letter* are called the *believer's rule of life*. He tells us that " it is implied;" this brings to my mind an old woman, who had been long contending for this *letter rule*; being afked *to give a reafon of the hope that was in her:* on fufpicion of her having none, replied; " You will find my experience in fuch a verfe of Jeremiah's prophecy;" hinting that it was implied there. Which ferved to convince the inquirer that fhe had no hope but what ftood on the paper. I fuppofe all the *experience* of the devil is implied in four texts of Scripture; one fays, *he is curfed above all cattle*; another, that *he believes and trembles*; another, that *he is caft down to hell*; and another, that *he is referved in everlafting chains under darknefs unto the judgment of the great day,* Jude vi. But the devil has another experience befide this, which will ftick clofe to him, and be like a thoufand hells within him, when every letter of Scripture text will be burnt up; when

when the *killing letter* has slain the reprobate, it has done it's office; the living Word that abides for ever, which is in the hand of the Spirit, and which dwells in the saints of God, will be *settled in heaven,* and abide for ever there. The professor must have Christ in him the hope of glory, if ever he arrives safe to the happy enjoyment of God in heaven. People, who have no hope but in the written letter of Scripture, will find that the flood of wrath and the final conflagration will leave them without an anchor in that storm; and I am persuaded that the *believer's rule of life* must be found in his heart also, if ever he lives with God in heaven. If the believer's rule be *implied* in the *ten commandments,* according to this gentleman's letter, I believe it would lie there long enough before he would find it out. To *put on the Lord Jesus and walk* in him; to put off the *old man* daily, and to put on the *new man,* which is *created in righteousness and true holiness*; to *follow Christ in the regeneration*; to *mortify the deeds of the body* by the Spirit; to deny self, and take up the cross daily; to stand fast in gospel liberty, and not be entangled with the yoke of bondage; to renounce all confidence in the flesh, and rejoice in Christ Jesus; to hate one's own life, or be unworthy of the Saviour; to walk in the Spirit, in order to escape the fulfilling of the lusts of the flesh; to know that the *strength of sin is the law*;

and that it is the miniſtration of death and condemnation; are things that, if they are implied in the ten commandments, they would lay there, concealed from the believer, to all eternity, if the myſtery of faith had not revealed them, or the *goſpel, that brings life and immortality to light*, had not brought them to light alſo. When *Moſes is read, the vail is upon their heart*, 2 Cor. iii. 15. By the law is the knowledge of ſin, but it brings not the *path of life* to light; *that is the new and living way*, Heb. x. 20. and is revealed from another quarter; *God, who commanded the light to ſhine out of darkneſs, hath ſhined into our hearts to give the light of the knowledge of the glory of God, in the face of Jeſus Chriſt*, 2 Cor. iv. 6.

I cannot find it in my heart to criticiſe the reaſons that you aſſign, becauſe you have not addreſſed me, as ſome have, with inſolence and lies; but you ſeem as deſirous of information, as you are to inform me, or ſet me right; therefore, without taking much of your letter to pieces, I will endeavour to make it appear, that the believer in his liberty is in no " ſenſe of the word an *outlaw*," nor yet *without law*; for he is in no wiſe excluded from any benefit that ariſes from the law, and yet he is not under the law *but under grace*, Rom. vi. 14.

Paul ſays *To them that are without law* [I became] *as without law*, (*being not* WITHOUT LAW TO to God *but* under the law to Christ), Rom. ix. 21. Hence it appears that the believer is not without law to God. And, as I have long made it my ftudy to confider the believer's laws, I will endeavour to bring them forth, and fet them in as fair a light as I am capable of, and fee whether they amount to what is called Antinomianifm, or whether they amount to real divinity; becaufe Paul fays, we *do not make void the law through faith.*

Wifdom affirms *whofo defpifeth the word fhall be deftroyed; but he that feareth the commandment fhall be rewarded*; and then tells us that *the* law *of the* wise *is a* fountain of life, *to depart from the* snares *of* death, Prov. xiii. 13, 14. Let it be obferved that Wifdom's *wife man,* who is always oppofed to the *fool,* is, in New Teftament language, the *believer,* who is oppofed to the *infidel*; and this *law* is emphatically called the *law* of the *wife,* which is the fame as the *houfehold of faith,* being their law in particular, as belonging to none elfe; and it is called a *fountain of life.*

A fountain is fupplied from its own fpring, and yields its contents to fupply the *poor and needy* when they feek water and there is none elfewhere, and their *tongue faileth for thirft,* that they may drink and not famifh, or die by famifhing. So this *law of the wife is a fountain of life,* to *depart from the fnares of death.* Can this *law of the wife*

B 3 be

be the ten commandments, which are affirmed by some to be the believer's only rule of life? *I trow not.* Paul tells us *the letter killeth,* 2 Cor. iii. 6. that it is the *law of death,* Rom. viii. 2. that the *law worketh wrath,* Rom. iv. 15. and is the *ministration of death and condemnation,* 2 Cor. iii. 7. 9. Nor does our faith in Christ alter the nature of the law, or make it to us what it was not before. It is the *yoke of bondage,* and *gendereth to bondage* still; hence we are exhorted to *stand fast in our liberty, and not be entangled again with that yoke of bondage,* Gal. v. 1. it still retains its binding nature, even to the believer, and will entangle him again if he looks to it for help. This *rule of life* (as some term it) is still a *killing letter;* hence God declares, that *we are delivered from the law, that being dead,* wherein we were held, *that we should serve* [him] *in newness of spirit, and not in the oldness of the latter,* Rom. vii. 6. If the law be a *killing letter,* and the law of death, it cannot be a *fountain of life;* by which the *wise man departs from the snares of death.* We know that *sin is a transgression of the law,* and that where there is *no law* there is *no transgression;* and that *death* is the *sentence* of the law; if so the *commandments* are the *snares* that hold the sinner in the *arms of death.* The first *snare* that entangles a *thief* is the *law;* and if he is left to the mercy of that, it will serve him as the spider does the fly in the web, never let him go till it has killed him;

it

it is a *killing letter*, and fo all will find it that weave the fpider's web; no web can be woven that will cover the foul on that loom; *the commandment is exceeding broad.* Nor can we fuppofe that our calling *the miniftration of condemnation* the *rule of life* will alter this matter, or turn a *killing letter* into a *living fountain*; for that law gives no life, therefore it can be no part of this law of the wife. *Had there been a law given that could have given life, verily righteoufnefs fhould have come by the law,* Gal. iii. 21. This *law of the wife,* that is, a *fountain of life,* to *depart* from the *fnares of death,* is what Paul calls *the miniftration of the Spirit* oppofed to *miniftration of death,* 2 Cor. iii. 11. Solomon's *fountain of life* is Paul's *miniftration of the Spirit;* and Solomon's *fnares of death* is Paul's law of death. The wife man's *law of life* is the fame as the living water that the Saviour gives, *that is in the believer* as a well of *water fpringing up into everlafting life,* John iv. 14.

Bleffed be God for ever, it is a *fountain of life* indeed, by which the poor believing finner *departs from the fnares of death,* and that for evermore; or, to fpeak in the apoftle's language, *The* LAW *of the* SPIRIT *of* LIFE *in* CHRIST JESUS *hath made me* FREE *from the* LAW *of* SIN *and* DEATH, Rom. viii. 2. that is, the law of the Spirit of life in Chrift has made me free from the law of fin that works in my members, and from the *law* of Mofes, which is the miniftration of death. We may call

this

this *law of the wife the believer's only rule of life*, without talking nonsense.

But perhaps my unknown friend may ask why this *dispensation of the Spirit* is called a *law?* To which I answer; first, because of its *binding power*, the *cords* of *everlasting love*, the *bond of peace*, and the *girdle of truth*, will hold the soul faster than all the lifeless commandments in the world, whether they be from heaven or of men. 2*dly*, It is called a *law*, because of its *constraining* power—the *love of Christ constrains us*, says Paul; it is a powerful constraint from evil, and mightily influences the mind to that which is good. 3*dly*, Because of the obedience it produces; the Blessed Giver of this law *circumcises our hearts, that we may love the Lord our God with all our heart and with all our soul, that we may live*, Deut. xxx. 6. It produces the *fruits of the spirit*, which is evangelical obedience; we are *taught of God to love one another* by the *love of God shed abroad in our hearts*, which is attended with *filial fear that keeps us from departing from God*, Jer. xxxii. 40. *God directs our work in truth by it*, Isaiah lxi. 8. and *works all our works in us*, Isaiah xxvi. 12. he *works in us* an inclining and moving power, *both to will and to do, and that of his own good pleasure*, Phil. ii. 13. Well may this be called the *law of the Spirit*, when it produces such *spiritual obedience*; well may the *desire of the righteous when it cometh be called a Tree of Life*,

Life, Prov. xiii. 12. feeing it produces love, joy, peace, meeknefs, temperance, &c. This *law of the wife* is called a *fountain*, becaufe it plays all its productions high enough to reach the fpring from whence it is fupplied; evangelical obedience fpringing from the Spirit of life and love, directed to the glory of God as the believer's chief end, makes the affembly of the faints like *a garden enclofed, a fpring fhut up, or a fountain fealed*, Song iv. 12. This law of the Spirit of life produces more real obedience to God in one hour than ever hath been produced by all the *living rules* that have been drawn by human wifdom from *killing fnares*. This law of the wife is *Chrift's yoke that is eafy, and it is his burden that is light*, Matt. xi. 29, 30. thofe fouls that are under this are *the circumcifion that worfhip God in the Spirit, rejoice in Chrift Jefus, and have no confidence in the flefh*, Phil. iii. 3. God writes *this* law on our hearts, *and in our minds does he put it*, Jer. xxxi. 33. This is the *law that goes forth of Zion* (not from Sinai), *and is the word of the Lord that went from Jerufalem*, Micah iv. 2. and thofe that receive it are the *people that keep the commandments of God and the faith of Jefus*, Rev. xiv. 12. By this law are the fervants of God warned, and in keeping *this there is great reward*, for charity abideth for ever, Pfalm xix. 11. This is the *holy commandment* delivered unto us, from which legions have continually departed, 2 Peter ii. 21. becaufe it

was

was only *delivered to them* in the *letter of it*, not put into them as a *fountain of a life*. Hence *they begin in the Spirit*, or with the difpenfation of the gofpel, and *end in the flefh*, or under the *killing letter*.

The law of the wife may be called a *fountain of life*, becaufe it *quickens* the dead foul, and *raifes it* to a *lively hope*; it produces that *life* which the law promifed but could not give becaufe we could give it no obedience; but this law enables a foul to *live unto God*, to *live by the faith of the Son of God*; it produces a *lively motion* toward God; it is attended with *life* and *peace*, and enables us to *love God that we may live* eternally with him.

Thus, Sir, the believer is not without law to God, for God has written his law in his heart, and he is *under this law* to Chrift as his eternal *head, king*, and *ruler*. And I think this is *fpeaking as the oracles of God*, and preaching of it is doing the *work of an evangelift*, and making full proof of the miniftry, much better than telling poor blind fouls " to look with one eye to Chrift, who is our life, and with the other to the law, which is death;" and it is better than bringing *rules of life* from a *law* which is *the ftrength of fin*, 1 Cor. xv. 5, 6. or telling people that the *rule of life* is *implied* in the *killing letter*; or that it appears *from the fitnefs of things*; when we know that a *living foul* ferving God in the *oldnefs of the latter* are things

things that can fit no better than darkness and light; the *eye of faith* and a *blinding vail;* perfect *liberty* and a *yoke* of *bondage;* real love and a *gendering to fear;* a display of *mercy* and a *revelation of wrath;* one working friendship and the other the motions of sin and vengeance. Are these the *things that will fit;* or what is the *fitness* that rises from them? I should *like to hear that author again of this matter,* Acts xvii. 32.

In order to convince my friend farther that we *do not make void the law through faith,* or represent the believer *without law to God,* I will fetch in another law, *which is not another,* but a branch of this that has been considered; and it is a *branch* that debases the proud boaster, cuts up the self-righteous, exposes the fool, lays the legalist in the dust, exposes the blind guide, furnishes the spiritual soldier of Christ with weapons against him, and secures the whole glory of salvation to God, to whom it belongs, and to whom it must be given without reserve.

" By the deeds of the law shall no flesh be jus-
" tified, for by it is the knowledge of sin; but
" the righteousness of God without the law is
" manifested, being witnessed by the law and the
" prophets, even the righteousness of God which
" is by faith of Jesus Christ; for all have sinned
" and come short of the glory of God; being
" justified freely by his grace, through the re-
" demption

"demption that is in Christ Jesus; whom God hath set forth to be a propitiation through faith in his blood, to declare his righteousness for the remission of sins that are past, through the forbearance of God; to declare at this time his righteousness, that he might be just, and the justifier of him which believeth in Jesus."— *Where is boasting then? It is excluded. By what law; of works? Nay, but by the* LAW OF FAITH, Rom. iii. 26, 27. But what doth Paul mean by *the law of faith?* Does he mean the gospel, which is sometimes called *faith,* as Paul, who persecuted the saints in times past, is said now to *preach the faith?* No; for the gospel is the revelation and explanation of the *covenant of promise;* and all the *blessings* of it are the *free gifts* of God ;—Christ the covenant head,—the Spirit of promise, everlasting righteousness, everlasting salvation, life, and glory, are all the gifts of God, held forth in unconditional promises, which are all *yea and amen, to the glory of God,* and our everlasting salvation.

As all these things come *freely* from God,—from the *better covenant,* a covenant of promise,—made with Christ, and with his *seed in him,* and are purely free in their fountain, in their administration, and bestowed to a God dishonouring and hell-deserving people, irrespective of any work, worth, or worthiness in them, there can be nothing like a law in it ;—that is, there is nothing that binds with rigour to obedience, or that threatens damnation for non-performance; there is nothing in it that sets a man to *work for life, reckoning the reward* to be of *debt*; for God gives grace to make us obedient to the faith, and by grace he *preserveth* and *rewardeth* the *faithful*. The Lord *gives both grace and glory*, and will *display the riches of his grace in glory by Christ Jesus*: yea, even the kingdom itself is given of God in his good pleasure. Therefore I presume that the *word of faith* dwelling richly in us, the *spirit of faith* working powerfully, and the grace of faith working by love, purifying the heart, holding an imputed righteousness, and giving Christ a residence within us, is Paul's *law of faith*. For it is not hearing the gospel, nor imbibing a speculative knowledge of it, that will exclude boasting, but the *word, Spirit,* and *grace of faith,* when powerfully applied to the heart, will stop the sinner's mouth, and for ever silence him upon that head. If you ask why Paul calls this the law of faith?—I answer, because faith works by love, which is the *fulfilling* of the *law,* which is the end of the commandment, and lays *hold* of *Christ,* who is the *end of the law;* and puts on an *everlasting righteousness* adequate to the law; because it is Christ's obedience thereto, and because *he that believes hath everlasting life,* which was the greatest thing that the law ever promised,—and which that law could never give;

and

and because the believer has the *Spirit of holiness*,— as the law is holy;—by faith he is a *just man*, as the law is just;—a *good man*, as the law is good;— a *spiritual man*, as the *law is spiritual:* and thus the *righteousness of the law is fulfilled in us, who walk not after the flesh, but after the Spirit*, Rom. viii. 4. I will shew my friend that I have yet to speak on the saints' behalf, on the subject of their being not *without law to God*.

As Paul divides the *believer* from the *infidel*, and divides the laws between them also, applying the *law of faith* to the believer, and the *law of works* to the infidel, declaring that *whatsoever things the law saith, it saith to them that are under the law*, Rom. iii. 19. and those that are *under the law* are *under sin*, Gal. iii. 22. and *under the curse*, Gal. iii. 10. so James divides the *hearer* from the *doer*. He tells us that *God of his own will begat us with the word of truth*, that we should be a kind of *first-fruits* of his creatures; and then tells us to be *doers* of the word and not *hearers* only, deceiving ourselves. By *doing* he means the *works* or *fruits* of faith—*Shew me*, saith he, *thy faith without thy works, and I will shew thee my faith by my works;* and then adds—for if a man be a *hearer of the word and not a doer, he is like unto a man beholding his natural face in a glass, for he beholdeth himself and goeth his way, and straightway forgetteth what manner of man he was*. Here James compares the *gospel*

gospel preached to a *glass*, the light of which reflecting upon the sinner's conscience makes manifest the state of his soul; as Paul speaks—*but we with open face beholding as in a glass*, 2 Cor. iii. 18. so here the sinner *hates the light,* and goeth his way; he will come no more to it ;—this *glass* has *shewed*, and the *light* of it has *reproved his deeds*, therefore he hates it, and *goeth his way* into the world again, and so hardens his heart and sears his conscience, until all is forgot, and then he sinks into a deeper security; or, as the text saith, *he straightway forgetteth what manner of man he was : but whoso looketh into the perfect law of liberty, and continueth in it, he being not a forgetful hearer, but a doer of the work, this man shall be blessed in his deed,* James i. 25. Here is a law of *perfect liberty*, or a *perfect law of liberty*, to be *looked into,* and to be *continued in,* if a man will be *blessed in his deed.*

If my friend asks what this law of liberty is, I will endeavour to shew him. It is taken from the *law of release,* when the *jubilee trumpet* was to be founded, and liberty to be proclaimed according to the tenor of that law. *If thou buy an Hebrew servant, six years shall he serve, and in the seventh he shall go out free for nothing : If he came in by himself he shall go out by himself; if he were married, then his wife shall go out with him,* Exod. xxi. 23. Every poor elect sinner is like this Hebrew servant, *he has sold himself for nought,* Isaiah lii. 3. and
is

is *the servant of sin,* and under the *dominion of the law*—two hard masters indeed, who shew no favour; he that is under the *dominion of sin* is also *under the law* of death; he that is delivered from the *power of sin,* is *delivered from the law also,* as the apostle intimates, *sin shall not have dominion over you; but why? because you are not under the law,* which is *the strength of sin,* 1 Cor. xv. 56. *but under grace, which reigns through righteousness unto eternal life.* In this state of servitude the sinner lies till *the great trumpet be blown,* Isaiah xxvii. 13. and the *joyful sound* reaches his ears, Psalm lxxxix. 15. by which *Christ preaches deliverance to captives, and set at liberty those that are bruised* with this *yoke* of hard *service,* Luke iv. 18.

When the Hebrew *servant's liberty was proclaimed,* he was delivered from his master, from the command of his master, from the threatening of his master, and from the service of his master—he was a free man—he shall, says God, *go out free;* and yet this man, that went out at the year of jubilee, is, says God, *my servant,* Lev. xxv. 42. So the believing sinner is *delivered from the law, that being dead,* Rom. vii. 6. from the *command of the law,* Acts xv. 24. *for the letter killeth,* 2 Cor. iii. 6. from the *curse of the law,* Gal. iii. 13.—and from the *service of the law,* for he shall *serve in the newness of the Spirit, and not in the oldness of the letter,* Rom. vii. 6. He is a *free man: if the Son therefore*

fore shall make you free, ye shall be free indeed, John viii. 36. and yet he that is this *free man is Chrift's fervant,* 1 Cor. vii. 22. for though he is not UNDER *the law,* yet he is not WITHOUT *law to God, but under this law of liberty to Chrift, who has made him free indeed,* and he that *looketh into this law of liberty,* and continues in it, fhall be *bleffed in his deed.*

No doubt but many of the mercenary Hebrew mafters were grieved at this law of liberty; they were gauled and chafed in their minds to fee their flaves go out free. Hence we read that *Zedekiah made a covenant with all the people at Jerufalem, to proclaim liberty to their fervants unjuftly detained: That every man fhould let his man fervant or maid fervant, being an Hebrew or Hebrewefs, go free: that they fhould not ferve themfelves of them. When the princes and people heard of this covenant of the kings, they obeyed it, and let their fervants go free; but afterwards they turned, and caufed the fervants and the handmaids, whom they had let go free, to return, and brought them into fubjection as fervants and handmaids again.*

I made a covenant with your fathers, fays God, *that when the fervant had ferved fix years ye fhall let him go free, and you had now turned and done right in my fight, in proclaiming liberty; and ye had made a covenant before me, in the houfe which is called by my name, but ye returned and polluted my name, by caufing every man and maid-fervant whom he had fet at liberty at their pleafure to return, and brought them into* SUBJECTION.

C *Therefore,*

Therefore, thus saith the Lord, Ye have not hearkened unto Me in proclaiming liberty; Behold, I proclaim a liberty for you, saith the Lord, to the sword, to the pestilence, and to the famine, and I will make you to be removed into all the kingdoms of the earth, and I will give you into the hands of your enemies, and into the hands of them that seek your life, and your dead bodies shall be meat for the fowls of heaven; read Jeremiah chap. xxxiv.

He that leadeth into captivity must go into captivity, says John, Rev. xiii. 10. and so it was here, the masters hated the *Lord's release*—they refused to *break the yoke,* therefore God put their *necks under the yoke of the king of Babylon,* Jer. xxvii. 8. and left them in his service threescore and ten years, and then proclaimed a *jubilee* to them, which they were as glad to hear of as their poor servants had been before; as it is written, *when the Lord turned the captivity of Zion we were like them that dream*; but the deliverance that God proclaimed to them was more than *a dream,* though that was little better that they had formerly proclaimed to their servants: God's release of them was real, *which filled their mouth with laughter, and their tongues with singing,* insomuch, that the *heathens said the Lord hath done great things for them,* Psalm cxxvi. 1, 2. These *mercenary masters* are lively figures of many of our preachers—and itis with allusion to them that the inspired penmen often speak of *false apostles and*

and *deceitful workers*, who under the *vail of the law*, and the *influence of the devil transformed*, call the *everlasting gospel Antinomianism*, the preachers of it *Antinomians*, the powerful operations of the Spirit of it *enthusiasm*, and the liberty of it *licentiousness*; as if the Word, Spirit, grace, and ministers of the Lord, were the only instruments of Satan; and graceless men, the only infallible preachers of holiness, who under a false shew of it tempt God— bring forth the old yoke—lead the saints into bondage, pervert their way, and set their hearts to fretting against the Lord, Prov. xix. 3. Of this number are some—I may say *legions, for they are many*—that go from our *universities* and *academies*; who have no other qualifications for the ministry, authority in it, *credentials* for it, right to *live* by it, or to claim the *honour* of it, than that which is of men; they are *ministers of men and by men*. And among all the mysteries that puzzle the wise this is none of the least, that men of *worldly wisdom, which God calls foolishness*, 1 Cor. iii. 19. and *wise and prudent men, from whom he has hid the mysteries of his kingdom*, Matt. xi. 25. should be able with the help of that *wisdom that is earthly, sensual, and devilish*, James iii. 15. to turn carnal men into *ministers of the Spirit*, spiritual lords, *divines*, and *doctors of divinity*; but so it is, if we may credit all that we hear—but how it is done must remain a mystery, until he that has promised to *reveal the*

C 2

mystery

myſtery of iniquity reveal this alſo as a main branch of it. And who ſet theſe men to *heap to themſelves teachers* is alſo as great a myſtery. I know Paul bids Timothy commit his *doctrine to faithful men, that they might be able to teach others*; but to turn *infidels into faithful men* and divines is another thing. Paul ſpeaks of ſome in his days that acted as the Hebrew maſters did by their ſervants, who proclaimed liberty to them, and *ſubjected* them to ſervitude again; and calls them *falſe brethren, unawares brought in, who came in privily to ſpy out our liberty which we have in Jeſus Chriſt, that they might bring us into bondage, to whom we gave place by* SUBJECTION *no not for an hour; that the truth of the goſpel,* (or the freedom that Chriſt has promiſed to them that *receive the truth,* John viii. 32.) *might not continue with you,* Gal. ii. 4, 5. And what was the *bondage* that theſe ſpies, who came privily, brought in unexpectedly, wanted to bring them into? why they wanted to ſubject them to the COMMAND OF THE LAW, *which genders to bondage,* by telling them that they were *under the law* as a *rule of life.* There *roſe up certain of the ſect of the Phariſees which believed, ſaying that it was* NEEDFUL *to circumciſe the* believing Gentiles, *and to* COMMAND *them to* KEEP THE LAW *of Moſes,* Acts xv. 5. Here is the command to the believers—they were to keep the law of Moſes; to which Peter anſwers, *God who knoweth the hearts bear them witneſs, giving them* the Holy Ghoſt, even as he did to us, and put no difference between us and them, PURIFYING their HEARTS by FAITH. Now therefore why TEMPT ye God to put a YOKE upon the neck of the diſciples, which neither our fathers nor we were able to bear? Acts xxv. 8, 9, 10. The liberty which Peter here alludes to is the liberty of the Holy Ghoſt, which God had given them, which Paul calls the *law of the Spirit of life*, which made him *free from the law of ſin and death*—for *where the Spirit of the Lord is there is liberty*, 2 Cor. iii. 17. for, as David ſays, the Spirit of God is a *free Spirit*, Pſalm li. 12. The rule that Peter gives them is *faith, which purifies the heart*. The unbearable *yoke* that they were going to tempt God with, by galling the neck of the diſciples, was, *firſt*, the *needfulneſs of circumciſion:* 2dly, a *command to keep the law of Moſes*; and it is called *tempting God*, becauſe it was a reflection caſt upon his work who had purified their *hearts by faith*, and ſent his Spirit to govern and lead them into all truth—as if the *Holy Ghoſt* was not ſufficient to make them obedient, nor God's purifying their hearts a ſufficient purification, nor *faith* a ſufficient *rule*—without yoking them with the *killing letter* as the only rule of *life*. And as it was then ſo it is now—every man that refuſes to tempt God, and that will not bring forth this yoke, and that does not affirm that the *killing letter* is the *living man's only rule of life*, is an *Antinomian,*

mian, a licentious person, a *man in errors*, one that *makes void the law*, and is cried down by every blind watchman, though they cannot bring one text to prove that the believer is under the law as a rule of life; nor one text that calls Moses' law the believer's rule of life; nor one text from God's book to overthrow *this doctrine, this everlasting gospel:* Paul says, they know not what they say, nor whereof they affirm.

If it be urged the command, *thou shalt love the Lord thy God with all thy heart*, is still a yoke upon the believer's neck: it is answered, the *believer is not under the law, but under grace*—not an *heir of wrath, nor of the commandments*, but an *heir of promise*: and he is to take the commandment to the *promise*, which belongs to the *better covenant*; and he will find that God has promised to circumcise his heart, and that he *shall love the Lord that he may live.* Paul makes a difference between the *commandment* and *Christ*—I have *loved them with an everlasting love, and with loving kindness have I drawn*, is in a promise, and is better than a command: they SHALL *love me* is safer and better than DO *love me*; it comes from the *better covenant*, established upon *better promises* than conditional ones, *and is sure to all the chosen seed.*

I have considered *Solomon's conclusion of the whole matter, fear God and keep his commandments, for this is the whole duty of man*, Eccl. ii. 14. and have deliberately

liberately considered all that you have drawn from the text; and I have likewise considered Paul's comment on *Solomon's words*, which differs much from yours—*Now the end of the commandment is charity, out of a pure heart and of a good conscience, and of faith unfeigned; from which some having swerved have turned aside unto vain jangling, desiring to be teachers of the law, understanding neither what they say, nor whereof they affirm*, 1 Tim. i. 5, 6, 7. What Solomon calls the *conclusion of the whole matter* Paul calls the *end of the commandment*; which James calls *the perfect law of liberty*; which Peter calls the *gift of the Holy Ghost* and of *purifying faith*; which is the Saviour's *easy yoke* and *springing well*; which is Paul's *law of the Spirit of life*; Solomon's *law of the wise*; the prophets' *law that went forth out of Zion*; the apostles *law of faith*; Peter's *holy commandment* delivered unto us; and that end of the commandment, which is charity, out of an heart purified by *faith*, attended with a good conscience, which all *turn* from who *end in the flesh*, and give themselves up to *vain jangling*, or to talking about things which they understand not.

If my friend objects, and enforces the commands of Christ concerning hearing the word, attending the Lord's supper, &c. &c. it is answered, the *Spirit shall lead them into all truth*; and if the Spirit lead them not it is *serving in the oldness of the letter*, contrary to the apostle's doctrine— which he *received not of men, nor was he taught it*, but

but by the revelation of Jesus Christ, Gal. i. 11, 12. And if *purifying faith* be not the *rule* of the believer's actions or obedience to the commands of Christ, and if he be not *fully persuaded* by the *Spirit of faith* in *his own mind*, his *works* are sin; *whatsoever is not of faith is sin*, Rom. xiv. 23. to *the unbelieving there is nothing pure, their mind and conscience is defiled*, Titus i. 15.—nor does their obedience spring from that charity which is the end of the commandment, out of a *pure heart, of a good conscience, and of faith unfeigned*—but is a *swerving from it*. This is gospel that can never be overthrown; gospel which God ever has and ever will set his seal to; gospel which no hypocrite ever knew in the power thereof; gospel that shall never pass away, even when heaven and earth are both removed.

It will be expected that my unknown friend will send me, in his answer to this, from the word of God, an account of the bad effects, licentious practices, and libertinism, that this doctrine has produced in the saints of God; and likewise an account from Scripture of the superior holiness, fruitfulness, or usefulness, that has demonstrated itself in those who have *tempted God*, by putting the *commanding yoke* of the law upon the disciples' necks; or, as Paul says, *swerved from this end of the commandment*, which is charity out of a pure heart, to the study and practice of *vain jangling*, or *desiring to be teachers of the law*, knowing neither what they say nor whereof they affirm.

It is not to be wondered at that men love or desire to be teachers of the law; the letter is more superficial, it lays nearer home, and is within the compass of nature. But as for this mystery, to an unenlightened, unquickened, uninspired, unrenewed minister of the letter, it is too profound a depth; the *natural man receives it not, nor can he know it*, because it is spiritually discerned, and by the saints powerfully felt, but it will ever remain a *parable in the mouth of fools*, Prov. xxvi. 7. These are the *great things of God's law*, and *they are accounted a strange* thing, Hos. viii. 12. It contains all the *weighty matters* of the law *judgment, mercy, faith*, and the *love of God*, and teaches a man to do the *lesser matters* in *faith*, and under the constraining power of the Spirit of love and of a sound mind—found in the faith, and inspired with love, which will make a man obedient unto death—*love is strong as death*; and so those saints found it who *loved not their lives unto the death*, Rev. xii. 11. I come now to *another branch of this perfect law of liberty*—which is to be *continued in*, if a man will *be blessed in his deed.*

" Know you not, brethren, (for I speak to them
" *that know the law*), how that the *law* hath *domi-*
" *nion over a man* as long as he *liveth?* For the
" woman which hath an husband is *bound by the*
" *law to her husband so long as he liveth*; but if the
"   *husband*

"*husband be dead* she is *loosed from the law of her
husband*. So then, if while her *husband liveth* she
be *married* to another man, she shall be called
an *adulteress*; but if *her husband be dead she is
free from that law*; so that *she is no adulteress*
though she be *married* to *another man*. Where-
fore, *my brethren, ye also are become dead to the
law by the body of Christ, that ye should be married
to another, even to him who is raised from the dead,
that we should bring forth fruit unto God,"* Rom. vii.
1, 2, 3, 4. If Paul has any meaning I think it
amounts to this—*that the law has the same dominion
over the sinner, that expects life or help from it by his
own* obedience to the rules of it, as the husband
has over his wife by the law of marriage; and the
law communicates *bondage* to the soul, which the
soul naturally *genders to*, until the soul be pregnant
with horror, despair, and misery, just as a man
communicates seed to a wife, who brings forth a
still-born or *dead* child, which is the *worst of labours*
without any heir to satisfy the husband, as Paul
aims to prove—*for, when we were in the flesh, the
motions of sin, which were by the law, did work in our
members to bring forth fruit unto death*, Rom. vii. 5.
But when God tells the poor sinner, who is so fond
of *being Moses's disciple*, that *Moses my servant is
dead*, Joshua i. 2. and the soul is quickened to feel
and enlightened to see that the law is a *killing letter*,
the *law of death*, and the ministration of *condemnation*;

tion; and that the foul can, bring forth no fruit to God under its gendering bondage, no fruit but *fruit unto death* or *dead works*; the foul feeing a DEAD HUSBAND, and a *dead law*, that *cannot give life, the foul is loofed from that law*; nor is it an adulterefs, nor an Antinomian, though it be married to another man. For that law has no more power over fuch a foul than the *corpfe of Anna's hufband had over her, who had been a widow upwards of forty years, and had lived with an hufband but feven years from her virginity*, and was then waiting to be married to the *confolation of Ifrael*, Luke ii. 36. The way that the foul gets *releafed from that law is by the body of Chrift*. The foul fees that the law curfed the Saviour as well as the finner, and that the Lord died under the law; that it was the *law of death* to the Saviour as well as to the finner; and, finding Chrift raifed from the dead, it goes after him and unites with him, and is begotten to a *lively hope by his refurrection from the dead*; and Chrift formed in the foul the *hope of glory* is an *incorruptible feed* indeed, a precious fruit. Such are no *adulteresses* though they be *married to another man*. Nor do they deferve the name of *licentious Antinomians*, feeing the Holy Ghoft affirmeth that this is done that they may *bring forth fruit unto God*, Rom. vii. 4. namely, the fruits of the Spirit. If the rigorous hufband of a poor fimple woman be dead, according to Paul's doctrine,

doctrine, Rom. vii. 2. one would think that he could command her person, pinch her belly, and beat her back no more; and that the other man whom she had married had got the sole and whole command of her; I am sure he has by the laws of God, and by the covenant of wedlock, or else I know not who would *marry a widow*, to have her hunted with the commands of a ghost. However, if the *killing commandments of the dead husband* be the *believer's only rule of life*, who is espoused to Christ by faith, this is the case—*Moses, the Lord's servant*, has still the command and dominion over the *bride the Lamb's wife*, Rev. xxi. 9. And notwithstanding his being dead, as God affirms, yet he must manage the *household of faith*, and give the *only rule of life to the queen*, although she *be exalted to stand at the right hand of the king in gold of Ophir*, Psalm xlv. 9. If she be at the right hand of the king, they do her much wrong who place her at the foot of a servant; one would think that, *as he* was not *permitted to go into the promised land* (though he fain would), which was but a *faint type of heaven*, he could never have such power over the *house* or church of *Christ*, which is so often emphatically called *heaven*.

We are *under the law as the rule of life*, say some; then the *law of liberty is far from being perfect*. One would think that souls espoused to Christ, and married to him, *that they should bring forth fruit*

fruit unto God, were under no law but that of the *hufband*; or, as Paul fays, under the law to Chrift. And I am fure it is fo with fouls wedded to Mofes he has the whole command of them, for they are without the *fpiritual law of life* altogether: and furely the *fecond hufband* has as much right as the firft; if we allow *this man to be worthy of as much*, Paul fays, *he is counted worthy of more glory than Mofes, inafmuch as he who hath builded the houfe*, as Jacob *built the houfe of Ifrael by Rachel and Leah*, Ruth iv. 11. *is worthy of more honour than the houfe*, Heb. iii. 3. It is clear that all the fruit brought forth under Mofes was but *dead works*, or *fruit unto death*;—therefore he *built no houfe* or *houfehold* but that of the *bond woman*, who is affirmed to be *defolate*; and, with refpect to God, *fhe is faid to have no hufband*, Gal. iv. 27. and therefore all her offspring are a *baftard* race of *dead children*, dead in trefpaffes and fins, which are *funk* into the *fynagogue of Satan* inftead of a *righteous nation*, called *the living, that are to rife up and praife Chrift*, Ifaiah xxxviii. 19. Hence we learn that fouls under the law wedded to Mofes are not God's wife—they bring forth fruit unto death, not unto God—they are free from righteoufnefs. God fays, I am not their hufband—Mofes has full command of them—though he accufes them day and night; and Chrift himfelf always fends fuch fouls to the law, that they may not marry another
while

while the first husband lives. But when an *accusing Moses*, and his *killing law*, have executed their sentence of death on the soul, it is then dead; and if Christ quickens it and enlightens it, and it flies, as *Ruth did, to his skirt, if he spreads his skirt over it it is a time of love, and if he enters into a marriage covenant with such a soul* it becomes his own, Ezek. xvi. 8. He has the whole command of such, and the full possession of them; he has married the soul that was in a *state of widowhood*, and says *thy Maker is thy husband—thou shalt remember the reproach of thy widowhood no more.* Thus he marries the *widow*, discharges her *debts*, redeems the *mortgaged inheritance*, raises up the *name of the dead upon it, and does worthily in Ephratah, and is famous in Bethlehem*, Ruth iv. 11.

Paul tells us that he was *dead to the law—I through the law am dead to the law, that I might live unto God*, Gal. ii. 19. He tells us that when the commandment came sin revived, and he died; that *sin took occasion by the commandment, deceived him, and by it slew him*, Rom. vii. 9, 10, 11. One would think that, when a law has apprehended a transgressor, arraigned him, tried him, cast him, condemned him, executed him, and buried him, he was got out of the reach of that *rule of life*. Paul says the *law came to him*, it apprehended him, *sin revived*, he was found guilty—it *took an occasion by the law* to expose him to death, *deceived him*,

with

with respect to all hopes in it, and *slew him* by the sentence of it; that he *was dead* and *buried with Christ*, or *planted together with him in the* LIKENESS *of his death*. If so, one would have thought that it had done with him.

But, according to some, this killing letter, or moral law, has never done with the believer—they would make it like the *Popish law*, which makes a believer in Christ a heretic; condemns him, curses him with bell, book, and candle, and burns him to ashes, and yet pursues him still; if he goes to *purgatory* it follows him; if to heaven, it holds the *keys* of that; and at the judgment day there can be no favour or mercy without Popish absolution. So some handle the law of Moses; though it kills a man, and he is crucified, dead, buried, and *risen again through the operation of God*; yet the commandment that came, which deceived and slew him, is " still *his only rule of life*"—it is still binding, and if he goes into heaven itself it pursues him, for the " very angels round the throne are governed by it," as some affirm, which is strange, as *God's voice*, whether in the law or in the gospel, is declared to be *to the sons of men*, Prov. viii. 4.

It has been a puzzling matter to me to find out what it is that appears in Moses' ministry, with respect to success, that makes people so eager to copy after him. He *led the people forty years in the wilderness*

wilderness it is true, but he was so far from exceeding the apostles and evangelists in success, with respect to *conversion* work, that he declares *God hath not given you an heart to perceive, and eyes to see, and ears to hear unto this day*, Deut. xxix. 4.—and calls them *a perverse generation, a nation void of counsel, and children in whom is no faith*, Deut. xxxii. 20. And we know that their *carcases fell in unbelief twenty thousand together.* Yea, and the Jews for rejecting of Christ and cleaving to Moses were destroyed by infinite numbers, and with an infinite destruction; and a *Pharisee*, who is the greatest advocate for the law, *is farther from the kingdom of God than publicans and harlots*; and if *Moses be but read the vail is upon their hearts, nor can it be taken away till they turn to the Lord.*

No fruits are brought forth under the law but *wild grapes, wild figs, untimely fruits, dead works, mercenary* and *eye service*, and fruits unto death; and all spring from the base principles of *slavish fear;* done to get a name or *to be seen of men,* to merit heaven, and bring God in debtor to them: their works spring from the fear of a condemned criminal, which is the worst of *roots*, and are directed to *self*, the worst of *ends*; hence *Israel is said to be an empty vine* (not united to Christ the true vine), *therefore he brings forth fruit to himself,* Hosea x. 1. whereas the Christian finds *that from God is his fruit*

fruit found, Hof. xiv. 8. and inftead of bringing forth *fruit to himfelf* he muft *deny himfelf daily.*

With refpect to its "ufefulnefs to inftruct the children of God," it may be anfwered—believers are not without teachers; *the Lord their God teaches them to profit*, Ifaiah xlviii. 17. He teaches them by *the Spirit of love*, 2 Tim. i. 7. *to love him*, Deut. xxx. 6. Yea, *and they are taught of God to love one another*, 1 Thef. iv. 9. Chrift, the great prophet of the church, teaches them alfo. It is not now, *remember the law of Mofes my fervant—* but it is, *this is my beloved Son, hear ye him. All thy children fhall be taught of the Lord, and great fhall be the peace of thy children*, Ifaiah liv. 13. The Spirit of God, *the anointing which ye have received of him, abideth in you; and ye need not that any man teach you*, if he be a *minifter of the letter*, or one that brings *rules of life* from the *fnares of death: but, as the fame anointing teacheth you of all things, and is true, and is no lie, and even as it hath taught you, ye fhall abide him*, 1 John ii. 27. The grace of God, that bringeth falvation, *teaches them to deny ungodlinefs and worldly luft, and to live foberly, righteoufly, and godly in this prefent world*, Titus ii. 11, 12. The believer's own *reins*, when God *tries him*, *inftruct him in the right feafon*, Pfalm xvi. 7. The *heart of the wife*, being a *new heart*, which contains a *new fpirit, teacheth his mouth, and addeth learning to his lips*, Prov. xvi. 23. Thus the chil-
D   dren

dren of God are not without teachers, nor yet without divine and infallible teachers. And I would to God that the saints would attend a little more to their divine teaching; they would not *stumble upon the dark mountains,* be tossed about with every *blind guide* and wind of doctrine, and go hood-winked, *groping for the wall at noon-day,* as numbers of them do. But, alas, alas! instead of searching *the Scriptures,* as they are commanded to do, *which are able to make them wise to salvation, through faith that is in Christ Jesus,* they load their shelves, and stuff their heads with the notions of what are called *the fathers*; when, if they would try them by God's standard, they would find that not one half of their notions would *stand the touchstone* of *God's word.* If believers were to go to the great infallible Head and Prophet of the church by humble prayer, they would find their *judgment* better *informed,* their *thoughts* more *established,* and their *hearts* more firmly *fixed,* than ever they will be by reading a thousand *folio volumes* of such *mungrel divinity,* dashed with whole bowls of popery; where you may hunt for seven years and never find one page that can, in the strictest sense, be called *the everlasting gospel,* Rev. xiv. 6.

There are libraries, consisting chiefly of ancient books, that cost fifty thousand pounds, and I would not go fifty steps to call them all my own if stripped of that *despised book called the Bible,* and a few a few more that I could name, which were written by our own divines. I am fully perfuaded that every believer may get divinity more pure from adulteration, more *powerful,* more *fatisfactory,* more *eftablifhing,* by humble prayer to Chrift Jefus, in one hour, than ever he will get from all thofe authors that are called the fathers, who were as *blind as bats,* and their *writings* as full of *confufion* as a gentleman's *garret* is *full* of *lumber.* If a man *lack wifdom let him afk it of God, who giveth liberally and upbraideth not, and it fhall be given him,* James i. 5.

It is when men get *cold* to God—*dead* to ftudy—*powerlefs* and *faithlefs* in prayer—fhy of the Lord—at a *diftance* from his throne—and *beneath* heavenly mindednefs, and *void* of heavenly meditation—that they fly to thefe fathers inftead of flying to the FATHER OF ETERNITY, where wifdom, mercy, and comfort may be got; for *he is the Father of all mercies, and God of all comfort,* 2 Cor. i. 3. and I know that he will *withhold no good thing from them that walk uprightly,* Pfalm lxxxiv. 11.

As to the " letter of the ten commandments being an infallible rule of direction," is anfwered thus—they *lead to the* UNITY OF GOD; that law prohibits *idol worfhip* and all *covetoufnefs,* and *commands love to the neighbour*; but we are neither to *ferve God* nor *worfhip God* in the *oldnefs of the letter*; he *will be worfhipped in fpirit and in truth,* and *ferved in the newnefs of the fpirit alfo:* it is he that caufed the *light to fhine out of darknefs, that fhines into our hearts, and gives us the light of the knowledge of the glory of God in the face of Jefus Chrift.* God's *worfhip,* and God's *fervice,* are to be performed under the Spirit's influence; God is *a fpirit, and they that worfhip him* MUST *worfhip him in fpirit and in truth.* Although the law forbids covetoufnefs, the power of it will never make any man hate it—*the law is weak through the flefh*; the law of unfeigned faith, that works by love out of a pure confcience, will make a man hate covetoufnefs. *Pray for us,* fays Paul, *for we truft that we have a good confcience in all things, willing to live honeftly,* Heb. xiii. 18.

God has not left his people "without fufficient directions," nor yet without a director. *In all thy ways acknowledge God, and he fhall direct thy paths,* Prov. iii. 6. *Wifdom is profitable to direct; I will direct their work in truth,* fays God; *and I will make an everlafting covenant with them,* Ifaiah lxi. 8. It is *not in man that walketh to direct his fteps,* Jer. x. 23. *I will inftruct thee, and teach thee in the way which thou fhalt go—I will guide thee with mine eye. Be not like a horfe or a mule that have no underftanding,* Pfalm xxxii. 8, 9. *I will bring the blind by a way that they know not; I will lead them in paths that they have not known; I will make darknefs light before them,*

them, and crooked things straight: these things will I do unto them and not forsake them, Isaiah xlii. 16.

Sending the *citizens of Zion* to *Sinai* for *rules of life and direction,* is a contempt of *mount Zion, and of the heavenly Jerusalem, to which the Spirit of God leads all believers,* Heb. xii. 2 2. and is no less than a contempt of the *King of saints, whom God hath set on that most holy hill.* Making the letter the *only rule of life,* is *sending the saints wrong, forasmuch as the Lord hath said unto them, they shall henceforth return no more that way,* Deut. xvii. 16. *They have compassed that mount long enough,* Deut. ii. 2, 3. Moses *is dead and buried,* Joshua i. 2. Joshua is *to take the lead.*—It is *bewitching the people,* Gal. iii. 1. it is *sending them* to the *old yoke of bondage,* Gal. v. 1. which is a contempt of the *Saviour's yoke,* Matt. ii. 29. it is *turning their back upon grace,* Gal. v. 4. it is *abusing their liberty,* Gal. v. 1. it is *making Christ of none effect to them,* Gal. v. 4. and that he should profit them nothing, Gal. v. 2.

Elijah, who *travelled forty days into the wilderness* in order to go to *Horeb,* instead of going to *mount Zion,* was *asked* twice, by *way of reproof,* first in a storm, and then by a still voice, WHAT DOST THOU HERE, ELIJAH? 1 Kings xix. 9. 13. which was *attended* with an *earthquake,* a *whirlwind,* and a *fire;* God would not take him to heaven from that mount, though he requested to *die there;* that is *not the new and living way,* Heb. x. 20. he must go back to the *Holy Land,* over the river *Jordan again*, and into the *plains of Jericho*, where *Joshua*, typical of our Captain, *first took the lead, before the fiery chariot appeared to take him to heaven*, 2 Kings ii. 11.

Nor can *sending living souls to a killing letter for rules of life* be any way promotive of *fruitfulness*. There can be *no fruit brought forth to God's glory* without an *union*, by the Spirit of love, to Chriſt *the living vine: the branch cannot bear fruit of itſelf*. No *good fruit till the corrupt tree be made good* by grace;—*make the tree good and his fruit will be good; a good tree cannot bring forth evil fruit*. No *good works* without *faith; whatſoever is not of faith is ſin:* no *honeſt labours* without *love:* no *ſpiritual fruits* without the Spirit of God produce them : no works done *acceptable to God*, unleſs he *work in us both to will and to do them*

Nor does this doctrine " remove the bounds of the church, nor leave her without her encloſures," unleſs it can be proved that *God's putting his laws in their hearts, and writing them in their minds, giving them a new heart and a new ſpirit ; putting his fear within them, and promiſing they ſhall not depart from him* ; holding them *in his hand ſo that the gates of hell cannot prevail againſt them*; cauſing them *to walk in his ſtatutes, to keep his judgements and do them* ; being *a wall of fire round about them*, placing *ſalvation for walls and bulwarks*, and *keeping them by his mighty power through faith*; can be called " removing

ing the bounds and taking away the enclosures of the church." And I think it is a pity that such a *dispensation of superabounding grace*, the *ministration of God's eternal Spirit*, should find no more *favour* in the eyes of poor miserable sinners, nor any better *name* than that of Antinomianism. For my part, I believe it will go by another name at the *restitution of all things*; for, if Christ *restores all things*, he will doubtless *restore* his *own gospel* to its proper name.

As for " correcting unruly Christians by the law," I believe *the saint's law is written on the fleshly tables of every believing heart by the Spirit of God;* and that *Christ dwells in them by faith;* and that he *keeps* his royal *court* in mount Zion for all his *friends*, as he is crowned king there; but, as for Sinai, it is his court of judicature; he appears there as the judge of all. We are to *apprehend* the *unruly*, and take them to the royal court, and to the *bar of equity*; and *appeal*, as Paul *did*, to God and to conscience in God's sight: and when the unruly feels the force of faithful *reproof*, backed with the *Scriptures of truth*, and seconded by his *own conscience*, it will be more *mortifying* and *humbling* to him than flogging him with all the scourges that can be brought from the *ministration of death*. This never brought a *sinner to Christ*, nor *restored a backslider*; it is with the *cords of love* that God leads a soul to the Saviour; and by the same is the backslider restored.

restored. *I will heal their backslidings; I will love them freely*; Hosea xiv. 4.

Your " enforcing the command *to love God,* calling it the *believer's rule,* that must ever remain binding," is not *speaking as the oracles of God.* We know that the law commands us to love God; and we have received favours enough to bring us in debtors so to do; but the *carnal mind is enmity against God; it is not subject to that law, nor can be.* There is nothing that the law demands but what the gospel gives; and there is nothing that the law commands that it helps us to perform, nor does it afford strength, life, love, holiness, mercy, inclination, or power, to enable us to give it its dues.

I know " we are commanded *to walk in love as Christ hath loved us*; but we must settle things on their own proper basis. The end of the commandment is charity; but where do we get this charity or love?—why, it is shed abroad in our hearts by the Holy Ghost, which is GIVEN unto us. If it is given, it is from the covenant of promise, not from the covenant of works;—if salvation be of grace in every part, it is no more of works in any part. Love is the basis of a covenant of grace—I have loved thee with an everlasting love; the gift of Christ is the wonderful effect of it—God so loved the world that he gave his only begotten Son. It is with loving-kindness

ness that God draws us to Christ—no man can come unto me, except the Father which hath sent me draw him. Love is the bond of the everlasting covenant.—*My loving-kindness I will not utterly take from him, nor suffer my faithfulness to fail.* Love is the *bond of eternal union* between Christ and his church.—Thou, O Father, hast loved them as thou hast loved me, John xvii. 28. Love is the bond of heartfelt union between the Lord and us—*he that dwelleth in love dwelleth in God, and God dwelleth in him,* 1 John iv. 16.—and it is called the *love of God perfected in us*—not our love, which is of the law; for it is said *not that we loved God, but that he loved us.* And whoever sent men to preach, who can make no difference between the *law that worketh wrath,* and love which casteth out *fear,* which the law *genders*; no difference between the *killing letter* and the *bond of the everlasting covenant?* Let love stand upon its own bottom, fix it not on the letter of the law. The law reveals the wrath to come—it is God's magazine which contains all the *treasures of hail reserved against the day of battle and war,* Job xxxviii. 22. And who could ever have thought that the only rule of life for believers could be fetched from the *ministration of condemnation,* 2 Cor. iii. 9. the *snares of death,* Prov. xiii. 14. the *voice of words,* Heb. xii. 19. the *law that worketh wrath,* Rom. iv. 15. the
killing

killing letter, 2 Cor. iii. 6. the *law that is against us*, Col. ii. 14. the *adversary that delivers us to the judge to be cast into prison*, Matt. v. 25. a *law that furnishes the sinner with an accuser before God*, John v. 45. that *is contrary to us*, Col. ii. 14. that *cursed the Saviour himself, though innocent*, Gal. iii. 13. because he *undertook for his friends*. A *fiery law*, Deut. xxxiii. 2. a *fire kindled in God's anger*, Deut. xxxii. 22. *seven thunders that are to utter their voices*, Rev. x. 3. a *shower of snares, fire and brimstone, and an horrible tempest*, Psalm xi. 6. *a fire that shall burn to the lowest hell*, Deut. xxxii. 22. But so it is; and every preacher that does not *bind this grievous burden* upon men's shoulders; that does not *turn aside to vain jangling*; that refuses to *tempt God* by putting this *yoke* upon the *disciples' necks*, which none are able to bear; is an *erroneous man*; a man of a *bad spirit*; one that *makes void the law*; and is (as I have been often called) *a stinking Antinomian:* God be merciful to such men! I have no other *glass* to view them in but the scriptures of truth and my own experience. And, as God liveth, I do believe, if *fifteen* out of *twenty* of our present preachers, who are called *gospel ministers*, were to see themselves as I see them in the light of God's word, that they would wish they had *never been born*; *curse the day* in which they took upon them the *office of the ministry*, and wish
it

it to be *blotted out from the number of the months*, Job iii. 6. But, alas, alas! there are none who think themselves sufficient for *these things* but those of no understanding! A blind man knows not how to go to the city, Eccl. x. 15. A blind *man beholdeth not the way of the vineyards*, Job xxiv. 18.

This very polite letter of yours, Sir, has drawn into public print what I never intended to make public. I have suffered so much by what I have before advanced, that I intended to have kept these truths close between God and my own soul; who was pleased, unless I am deceived (without the help of any author) to lead me into them. I have suffered a deal for what I have already advanced from the pulpit and the press of these matters; and, for my part, I have not one single doubt of the whole of them being the truths of the everlasting gospel of Christ Jesus. But I have been termed a man of a bad spirit; a dangerous man; an erroneous man; a stinking Antinomian; a contentious man; a man of controversy; a man of pride and reservedness, putting his own constructions upon scripture; a bully; a singular man, who wants to represent all other ministers as *neuters*, and himself all in all.

Old women have pursued me with *twopenny, fourpenny*, and *sixpenny pamphlets*, of their own manufactory; a boy crying them from one *chapel door,*

door, where I preached, to the other; and their *squibs* have been sent to *Portsmouth, Bristol, &c.* wherever they heard that my books were sold. Ministers, behind the curtain, (who pretended friendship to me) have told these *old wives* what *brandy, meaning strength,* to put into their *fables—* what *sugar, meaning candour,* to use—and what *gaul, bitterness,* or *wormwood,* to withhold.

I was asked to go to Bristol by a gentleman (whom I cautioned to have nothing to do with me, as I was so dangerous a man,) who would insist upon my going thither; and without my desire, had me down. The poor people had been prejudiced to that degree that they expected to find me a minister of satan. The *parson-maker* levelled his artillery from the pulpit till he was quite out of breath, and set off for London. Another, in obedience to the Rev. R—— H——, refused to invite me to his pulpit, or to give me the right hand of fellowship. I wrote to Bristol since, offering to preach them a sermon, being engaged to go into Dorsetshire, but was denied; and all this sprung from a reverend gentleman of Plymouth, who has settled the matters of Bristol tabernacle so as to secure the pulpit against Antinomians. And the same gentleman (I shall not mention his name) has not acted like a brother, nor has he done the KINSMAN's part by me, but took some people to task for bringing my books

into

into Plymouth; and a reverend gentleman, who is now *settled at Walthamstow*, when he lived at Plymouth, made it his business to ridicule what I had written, in order to imbitter the people's minds against the doctrines; and no wonder, for, if these doctrines be true, what becomes of theirs? The Bishop of Spaw-fields Chapel lampooned me in public, till he got into the smoke of Sinai, insomuch, that some discerning people quite lost sight of him. Some of his people he excluded from the society because they came to hear me. His *mandates* went to Bristol, that they might not be infected; and to Lewes in Sussex also. Mr. Barnet refused me his pulpit, and threatened to leave the people if I were admitted; but a Baptist minister kindly threw open his meeting, which God filled with people, and my mouth with arguments. The congregation at Wooking, which God raised by me, must send me their final dismission before they could get any assistance from the Evangelical Association in London. The Reverend Mr. R. H. left his prelatic commands at *Chatham*, and twice since at *Greenwich*, never to admit me on peril of his final leave. If any of these *charges are false* let them plead their innocence; and if the doctrine be false let them be overthrown.

My friend may well ask—What is my sin? What have I done? Seeing some cry *one thing* and

and *some another* the assemblies are confused, and no account given of the cause of this concourse; and I can give none, unless it be for *this one voice that I cried among them;* touching the law, I said it is not the believer's 'rule of life. And this I do insist upon, that *bondage, hardness* of *heart, revealed wrath, enmity* against God, desperation, curses, hell and damnation, are the best things that men can fetch from the killing letter of the law of Moses; whether the man be a *believer* or an *infidel* it matters not. The law will pursue the believer if he goes there, Christ alone is his refuge; it will *entangle the believer, and yoke him again* if he looks for help there. The law is *not of faith,* but of *works;* it is *not of believing,* but *of doing: he that doth these things shall live in them,* is its language to the end of the chapter. *Works* are *works,* and *grace* is *grace;* the one is a *covenant of works,* the other a *covenant of grace:* one was *given by Moses,* the other came by *Jesus Christ.* The *covenant of works* was made with man; it belongs to Adam, and all his children in the flesh that bear his image: the *covenant of grace* was made with Christ, and all his seed in him. The one is *established* upon unconditional *promises,* the other upon the *conditions* of *dead men's performances;* and who would call this law *the believer's only rule of life,* he is to *walk* and *live by faith;* he is to worship and serve God in the newness of the Spirit, not in the oldness of the letter; he is to

walk

walk in love as Christ hath loved him. And it is plain that faith worketh by love, and is attended with divine life, which are *all the gifts of God in Christ Jesus;* they are received from *his fulness,* and wrought in us, and are no less than *the law of the Spirit of life in Christ Jesus, which makes us free from the law of sin and death.* If faith, life, holiness, and love, come from the *law of the Spirit,* why are they ingrafted upon the killing letter? and why is the believer sent to fetch his *rule of life* from that law which was once his *death warrant?* why this confusion? why this *turning things upside down?* The man that has got *the law of the Spirit of life in him* is the man to whom the Lord speaks by his Son— he speaks not to the believer out of the *cloudy pillar,* nor out of *thick darkness.* He has spoken to us in these last days by his Son; and it is to the believer that he thus speaks—*Hearken unto me, ye that know righteousness, the people in whose heart is my law.* A believer is a righteous man, made so by imputation; and *the law is not made for the righteous, but for the lawless and disobedient,* 1 Tim. i. 9. God speaks to the children of the flesh in the law. Now *we know that what things soever the law saith, it saith to them who are under the law,* Rom. iii. 19. But *the saints are not under the law, but under grace,* Rom. vi. 14. The law is a yoke of bondage for bond children, a covenant of works for proud workmongers,

mongers, and a *miniſtration of condemnation*, to curſe them for their pride and evil works.

As to what David ſays of *the law being perfect, converting the ſoul, and of its being a light to his feet and a lamp to his path,* it is ſoon anſwered. The killing letter never converted one ſoul to Chriſt yet; converſion conſiſts in turning a ſoul from darkneſs to light, from the love of ſin to love God with all his heart; which is attended with *faith, repentance,* and godly ſorrow, which flows from a ſenſe of God's love to him in Chriſt Jeſus; all which come from the covenant of grace. Faith is a coming to Chriſt, and the love that faith works by draws his heart as he goes; and both theſe are the free gift of God. Chriſt did not furniſh Saul with theſe *ſpiritual weapons, which are mighty through God to pull down ſtrong holds* from the killing letter. *I ſend thee Paul to turn ſinners from darkneſs to light, and from the power of Satan unto God, that they may receive* forgiveneſs of ſins, and *an inheritance among them that are ſanctified by faith that is in me,* Acts xxvi. 10. The brighteſt light that ſhines in the law comes from the eye of offended juſtice; it was in the flames of wrath that the law was given at firſt; it was *added becauſe of tranſgreſſion, and it is* in that awful light that ſinners ſee their own condemnation, as Saul and Balaam ſaw their own future deſtruction; and it is in that light that ſinners will ſee their endleſs miſery, who are ſaid *to lift up their eyes*

eyes in hell; but that light difcovers not the *path of life*, which is called the *path of the juft*. The light of the knowledge of the glory of God fhines in the face of *Jefus Chrift*, who is the *true light*, and the *everlafting light of all his people*; he that *believeth in me*, fays the Saviour, *fhall not abide in darknefs*.

David was not without the *law of faith*; he tells you he *believed, therefore hath he fpoken*; nor was he without *the law of the Spirit of life*, as appears by his prayer—*Take not thy Holy Spirit from me.* It was in *this law* that he *faw wonders*—as for the *ten commandments*, he prayed that *God would not enter into judgment with his fervant under them*, for he knew the *commandment was exceeding broad*. If the commandments afford fuch a deal of light to our feet, how comes it that our prefent advocates for them are fo exceeding blind? by them it appears that Paul's affertions are true, that the *vail remains untaken away in reading the Old Teftament*. I am bold therefore to affirm, Sir, that David and you have two different meanings.

With refpect to what you have heard " about my fpeaking lightly of the law," I believe you will find, in this my anfwer to yours, all that I have ever faid about it; and you muft judge for yourfelf whether I have fpoken the language of Scripture or not. If I have, lay the blame where it ought to be laid; *if a man confent not to the wholefome wholesome words of our Lord Jesus Christ, he is proud and knows nothing.*

However, as I am determined to publish this answer to yours, my accusers will have a fair opportunity to attack the doctrine. I have advanced on *the ground of truth*; I have fled to none of those poor shifts called *implications* and the *fitness of things*; I have used no *weapons* but those that I believe to be *spiritual*. They cannot have a fairer opportunity, nor a fairer field to meet me on, nor a smaller number to engage. If this be Antinomianism let them muster all their forces against it, prove it to be so, and overthrow it. I am open to *conviction, my conscience is not seared*, nor am I past *feeling*; and, if I cannot defend it by God's word, I will fly to no other shifts; and therefore I hope my opponents will not puzzle my brains with St. Basil, St. Augustine, St. Ambrose, Hermon Witsius, and saint nobody knows who.—*Jesus I know; but who are these?* For my part, I have not a single doubt but God will enable me to defend this doctrine; for I know it is the doctrine that he applied to me, and set my soul at liberty by. And as I am the Antinomian, according to their accusations, it lies with them to overthrow it, and prove their charge; and, if upon trial it be found to be the *everlasting gospel,* then *let them hear and say, it is truth,*

truth, Isaiah xliii. 9. and acknowledge that for the truth's sake I have suffered reproach.

These are the doctrines that have caused so many counsels to be taken—so many pulpits to be shut against me;—yea, in every place that I have gone, the people have been armed with prejudice against me as an erroneous man or an Antinomian—and have come to hear me as if I was a second *Simon Magus*, or *Judas Iscariot*, risen again. This has been the case at almost every place I have gone to except Portsmouth, where I met with such a kind reception from the ministers as I never met with before in my life. The Rev. Mr. *Horsey*, and his assistant, the Rev. Mr. *Phillips*, and the Rev. Mr. *Dun*, welcomed me to their pulpits in turn every night during my stay there, and treated me with the greatest respect and civility, which I mention to the honour of those gentlemen, and as a matter of wonder to me, it being what I had never been accustomed to.

I have not gone any country journey for the sake of gain, for my own people do not let me want; nor did I ever clear a shilling by any journey I took, because I have paid the same that I received for a supply in my absence, that I might not be *brought under the power of any*; therefore they could not refuse me their pulpits under an apprehension of my seeking filthy lucre. The reasons that they assigned were, that I held errors in
making

making void the *law*. And this has been carried so far, that, if any minister has happened to drop a word in the pulpit concerning the law, if he did not make it the believer's only rule of life, it has been called one of *Huntington's texts*; let them prove it is from Huntington, and I will endeavour to prove it is from heaven.

If the law of works be *binding* to the saints, as some affirm, then James's *law of liberty* is not *perfect*, nor can we be *blessed in our deeds* by *continuing in that*. If the law of works be binding, then " the law of the Spirit of life did not make Paul *free* from the law of death," unless it can be proved, that legal bondage and gospel liberty can stand together. If the believer be *under the law* as a rule of life, then he is *under the law* and *under grace* both at once; which Paul says he is not—he is not *under the law*, but *under grace*. If he be under the law as a rule of life, he has got Peter's *unbearable yoke* and *Christ's easy yoke* both on his neck at one time. The man that makes the killing letter his rule *walks by sight* not by faith; he *looks at the things that are seen*, not at the things which are not seen. He serves in the *oldness of the letter*, not in the newness of the Spirit; he *worships God in the letter*, not in spirit and in truth; nor is he *free indeed*. I know the law will bring a man into bondage notwithstanding his grace, if *he stands not fast in the liberty wherewith Christ has made him free*;

free; nor does *the law of the wife, as a fountain of life,* cause a man *to depart from the snares of death;* or, as the Saviour says, *pass from death to life* by faith, because the believer, according to them, is still *under the snares of death*; he is still under the *law of death* as his *only rule of life*. This is called preaching the gospel, doing the work of an evangelist, being a minister of the Spirit, making full proof of the ministry; and every man that cannot turn the *law that worketh* wrath into a law of love; that cannot bring the living fruits of the Spirit out of the killing letter; that cannot turn *the snares of death* into rules of life; is an erroneous man and an Antinomian. Welcome reproach! welcome names! welcome Antinomian! These names bring no guilt on the conscience; they stop not up the new and living way between God and the soul; they seal not up God's book, nor bind the spirit of liberty. Election secures every minister in his station, and all the success that shall attend his labours. It has been observed that those, who have been the most forward at lampooning me for an Antinomian, have been the greatest novices in divinity; and, while they have been contending for the law as the only rule of life, they have preached the greatest confusion, discovered the greatest ignorance of the nature of the law, and have evidently appeared in the strongest bondage—*He that leadeth into captivity shall go into captivity*—he that *binds grievous burdens on other men's shoulders* goes a sure way to load his own back.

No wonder that legions are flocking back to Sinai; it is a proof that the *law is not dead to them*, nor they *to it*; they begun *in the Spirit* before they had been *killed by the letter*. Their *first husband*, it is to be feared, 'is *not dead*, therefore they are not *loosed from that law*; and being *adulteresses*, the *first husband* has taken them up and brought them back, not being *loosed from their old bond of wedlock*, nor favoured with *a writing of divorcement*; therefore, as a *wife of the first covenant*, the eloped *Lo-ruhamah* is brought back, Hosea i. 6. Hos. ii. 1, 2. but *Hephzibah*, the Lord's delight, whom he has espoused to himself, *if she goes back, will return again to her first husband*, saying—It was better with me then than it is now. Consider, Sir, and see if there be any thing that you want to make you holy or happy that does not come from the *law of the Spirit of life*; and whether any of these things come from the law of works; whether mercy, grace, hope, or help comes from that quarter: and take heed that you do not jumble these two covenants together. One is a covenant of works, the other of grace—one is the law of death, the other the law of life; bond children are under the law—free children are under grace; they that are under grace are under the blessing—those under

under the law are under the curse; one are heirs of promise, the other heirs of wrath; one are children of God, the other are children of the devil. The free-born children receive the inheritance freely, the bond-children work to earn it. *The gift of God is eternal life,* the *wages of sin is death.* And, in order to clear this doctrine from the charge of Antinomianism, I will inquire *what this law of the Spirit of life produces,* for we are told that the *gospel brings forth fruit,* Col. i. 6. Paul says *the fruit of the Spirit is love, joy, peace, long-suffering, gentleness, goodness, faith, meekness, temperance; against such there is no law,* Gal. v. 22, 23.

Now let us see what *the law of the wife,* which Solomon calls *a fountain of life,* produces. I think we shall find the same things springing from his fountain as comes from *Paul's law of the Spirit:* Solomon says *wisdom loves them that love her;* and that *love is better than a house full of sacrifices;* and that, if a man *would give all the substance of his house for love, it would be condemned:* here is what Paul calls *the first fruit of the Spirit;* the next is Joy : *the heart knows its own bitterness, but a stranger intermeddleth not with his joy.* PEACE; *wisdom's ways are pleasantness, and all her paths are peace.* LONG-SUFFERING ; the *patient in spirit are better than the proud in spirit.* GENTLENESS; be not *hasty to go out of his sight; stand not in an evil thing.* GOODNESS; the upright shall have *good things* in possession. FAITH;

in the fear of the Lord is *strong confidence*, and his children shall have a place of refuge. MEEKNESS; God scorneth the scorners, but he giveth grace to the *lowly*. TEMPERANCE; the righteous *eateth to the satisfying of his soul*. Thus the fruits of Paul's law of the Spirit are the same as those that spring from Solomon's *law of the wise*, which he calls a fountain of life: and remember the gospel is called the *ministration of the Spirit*, and the law is the *ministration of the letter*; the letter killeth, but the Spirit giveth life. Solomon's fountain of life is supplied from God in covenant, who tells us that all *his springs are in Zion*; therefore it is vain to expect help from Sinai. The *law of the Spirit* will remain what it is, notwithstanding men's legality; and the *ministration of the letter* will remain what it is, notwithstanding men's faith and love; one will ever give life, and the other will ever give death: the one will ever produce freedom, and the other will ever *gender to bondage*.

Those that have felt the bondage, wrath, terrors, and death, that the law works, will prize their liberty; and take heed how they approach that *blackness and darkness* again; but those that never felt its power can *play with it as with a bird*, for *they are alive without it*. It is in vain that ministers send men to Sinai in order " to promote holiness:" the works of the flesh are these—*adultery, fornication, uncleanness, lasciviousness, idolatry, witchcraft,*

craft, hatred, variance, emulations, wrath, strife, seditions, heresies, envy, murder, drunkenness, Gal. v. 19, 20. And will sending men to the law destroy these? Nay, says Paul, these *are the motions of sin, which are by the law that works in our members to bring forth fruit unto death,* Rom. vii. 5. Nor was the law manifested to *destroy these works of the devil*—but to make them appear *exceeding sinful;* nor does the law weaken sin but aggrevate it; for *the strength of sin is the law,* 1 Cor. xv. 5, 6. It is grace that makes the believer what he is, nor will the law ever make him better. *Those that came privily in to spy out the apostles liberty that they might bring them into bondage,* Gal. ii. 4. agree exactly with you in sentiment; for, if the law be binding to the believer, and he be *under it* as a rule of life, it is the same as what they enforced; namely, *it is needful to circumcise them, and command them to keep the law of Moses,* Acts xv. 5. they said this was *needful;* you say the believer is under this *necessity:* they called it keeping the law of Moses; and you call the *law of Moses the believer's rule of life.* There is no more difference between your assertions and theirs than there is between my two eyes. If you object that it is circumcision only that is called the yoke that was unbearable; it is answered, they were circumcised at eight days old, therefore the fathers could give very little account of the unbearable pain of it. The yoke consisted in this—*he that is circumcised*

circumcised is a debtor to do the whole law, circumcision is nothing and uncircumcision is nothing, but the *keeping of the commandments of God* is what is meant, 1 Cor. vii. 19. submitting to circumcision is rejecting Christ, *who was a minister of the circumcision for the truth of God, to confirm the promises made unto the fathers.* And submitting to *the yoke of keeping the law of Moses* is rejecting *Christ's yoke,* which consists of *faith* and *love* in the *Spirit.* The yoke therefore is this, it is needful to circumcise the believers, *and to command them to keep the law of Moses,* Acts xv. 5. and you say the law is *binding,* and *that the believer is under the law as his rule of life*; you might just as well have stuck to the *old text,* for it amounts exactly to the same, nor doth your different way of expression alter the matter. Their NEED of *keeping the law of Moses* is your BINDING LAW as *a rule of life*; it is the spirit of legal bondage that obliges and binds you; and it was the same that influenced those who made it needful; different names make no alteration in the things. Those men *tempted God by putting that yoke on the saints,* and *subverted their souls* by saying *ye must be circumcised and keep the law of Moses, to whom God gave no such commandment,* Acts xv. 10. 24. and they do no less than tempt *God and subvert the souls of believers,* who tell them *the law is binding, and that they are under it as a rule of life*—" for God has given them no such commandment," Acts xv. 24. Nor can men expect

pect that the broad *seal* of heaven should attend a ministry that *tempts God* and *subverts the souls of his saints,* when it is expresly said that *it seemed good to the Holy Ghost, and to the apostles, to lay on them no such burden,* Acts xv. 28. However, *this is the way which seemeth right unto a man, but the end thereof are the ways of death,* Prov. xiv. 12. it is turning people from *grace* to *works;* from the *liberty of the Spirit* to the *bondage of the law;* from the *law of the Spirit of life to the law of death.* Liberty and bondage, grace and works, Christ's yoke and the yoke of Moses, the *true light* and the *old vail,* death and life, can never stand together, one must give way; grace shall reign, and Moses must be subject. If a believer be a *new creature,* has a *new heart,* a *new spirit,* walks in the *new and living way,* and must *serve God in the newness of the spirit,* and *walk in newness of life,* old things must be done away: and if old things are done away the yoke of bondage is included among them, which Paul calls the *law of death,* or else the apostle's assertion cannot stand good; therefore if any man be in Christ he is a new creature; *old things are passed away, behold all things are become new,* 2 Cor. v. 17. and he that *sits upon the throne says* behold *I create all things new. God has granted us boldness to enter into the holiest by the blood of Jesus, by a new and living way which he hath consecrated* [or new made] *for us through the vail, that is to say his flesh,*

flesh, Heb. x. 19, 20. Take heed, Sir, that you despise not this new and living way; it is the old way that you contend for at present, which is *stopped up*; it is *hedged about with thorns*, namely, the *curses of the law*; and so poor sinners will find it, when, like Balaam, they fall before that *terrible sword of God that turns every way to keep the way of the tree of life*, Gen. iv. 24. none will ever get to God that old way; the sword that keeps the way of life destroys all *thieves and robbers that climb up any other way*, John x. 1. or dare *to look through, or gaze, where God has fixed his bounds*, Exod. xix. 21, 22, 23.

I know the law is holy, just, and good, because it defends a holy, just, and good God, and will certainly cut off and destroy for ever every adversary that is found under it; but though the law is holy yet it sanctifies none; it is just, but it justifies none; it is good, but it imparts no *goodness* to men: God is our justifier and sanctifier; and *Christ is our righteousness* and *sanctification*. God's *goodness* to us comes by grace; severity comes by the law; *behold therefore the goodness and severity of God: on them which fell, severity; but towards thee, goodness, if thou continue in his goodness: otherwise, thou also shalt be cut off*, Rom. xi. 22. with the sword *furbished* at that *armory*. It is the *fiery law* that gives the *sword of justice its flaming edge*; where there is *no law there is no transgression*; *sin* is the *transgression*

sion of the law, and the law is the transgressor's *adversary* that makes his crimes appear *exceeding sinful*, and *delivers him to the judge*—here lies its power; the *strength of sin is the law*. But with respect to our *obedience*, its lending us any help, pardoning of us, or justifying of us, *it is weak through the flesh*, Rom. viii. 3.

I would to God, Sir, that you would pray a little more over your Bible, or *ask wisdom of God*. When Paul says *the law is spiritual*, but I am carnal, *sold under sin*, Rom. vii. 14. he does not mean thereby that spiritual life, spiritual health, spiritual help, or strength, is communicated from thence. The law gives neither righteousness, life, hope, help, nor strength. The law is strong to destroy, but never was mighty to save, nor is help laid upon that. It is called *spiritual*, because it reaches to the thoughts of men's hearts, and curses them for a *lascivious look as being adultery itself*, Matt. v. 28. for *anger* as *murder in the abstract*, 1 John iii. 15. yea, if a man *break one command he is guilty of all*, James ii. 10. it casts him for *every idle word*; for all that is *more than yea, yea, or nay, nay*; it brings him into judgment; and both *heaven and earth shall pass away before one jot or tittle of that law shall fail*, Luke xvi. 17.

It is called *spiritual*, because it reaches to spirits, yea to the wicked *souls* of men and *devils* also; for they are under one *curse* — it reveals wrath, spiritual

tual death, damnation, and everlasting destruction, both to the bodies and souls of all them who die under it; and it will hold all rebellious spirits, whether men or devils, in the *prison of hell till they can pay the very last mite,* Luke xii. 59. which will be done when lying in goal can be called paying of debts. God says this *fiery law*, which is a revelation of wrath, *kindled in his anger*, shall burn *to the lowest hell.* Christ, our *passover*, was roasted in that fire, and it *made his heart like wax, it melted in the midst of his bowels*, Psalm xxii. 14. therefore take heed that thou attempt not to turn that ministration of death into rules of life. Cleave close to him that is *a hiding place from that north wind, and a covert from that tempest*, Isaiah xxxii. 2. In Christ Jesus thou shalt find refuge when God makes the *wicked as a fiery wheel, and persecutes them with all these storms*, Psalm lxxxiii. 13, 14, 15, but no where else.

If this be handling the law lawfully, and holding forth the word of life, as a faithful steward of the manifold grace of God; if this be rightly dividing the word of truth; if it be giving to each his portion in due season — a portion to seven, and also to eight; if it be doing the work of an evangelist; if it be preaching the gospel according to Christ's command; if it be handling the word faithfully as a minister of the Spirit; if it be acting like a workman that needeth not to be ashamed,

being

being approved of God;—in short, if this be *preaching the mystery of faith*, then where are legions of our present preachers got? and if this be the pure, unmixt, unadulterated gospel of Christ, what is nine parts out of ten of the doctrine that is delivered in our days under that name? and if this be error and Antinomianism, then WHAT IS GOSPEL?

I understand your hint, Sir; those speak it more plain who call me "in public a stinking Antinomian;" and this "doctrine antinomianism which leads to licentiousness." And I wish they would speak it plainer still; then they would appear in their proper colours, and be less capable of deceiving the simple. They must either prove this doctrine to be errors instead of truth, licentious antinomianism instead of gospel, or else acknowledge that their calumny amounts to this in the sight of God—that, instead *of walking in the Spirit*, and delivering people from *fulfilling the lusts of the flesh*, it leads them into it; that, instead of the *grace of God teaching men to deny ungodliness and worldly lust, and to live soberly, righteously, and godlily*, it encourages ungodliness, and a licentious way of living; and, instead of the *law of the Spirit making men free from the law of sin and death*, that it leads them into sin, the wages of which is death.—This is their reproach, and this is the meaning of it in the sight of God; and it is plain to an spiritual

ritual mind where this reproach falls; namely, on that God *who is gracious and merciful;* on that Saviour by whom *grace and truth came,* as if he was the minister of sin; and upon the *Spirit of grace,* who gives the *law of faith,* and who is the real giver of the *law of life,* it being emphatically called by the apostle his *law,* or *the law of the Spirit of life.* This, Sir, borders close upon the *unpardonable sin;* it is trifling *with the folds of infinite wisdom,* Eph. iii. 10. and with the *greatest dispensation* that ever heaven revealed to men, 2 Cor. iii. 8. It is making free with the *spiritual court,* from *which* there is no *appeal;* it is sinning against the last condescending lawgiver that ever appeared in this lower world. The Holy Ghost gives *that law of the wise that is the fountain of life;* he gives the *law of faith that excludes all boasting.* The Holy Ghost is the giver of the *law of life, that takes men from the law of sin and* the snares of *death.* It is this lawgiver that brings every blessing from heaven, testifies of Christ, and glorifies him on his throne; whose kingdom stands not in word, or in *rules of life* drawn from the letter of Moses' law, but in POWER, in *righteousness, peace, and joy,* in THE HOLY GHOST. To do *despite to the Spirit of grace* is *treading under foot the Son of God whom the Spirit testifies of,* Heb. x. 29. Sin against him, the Saviour *that saves to the uttermost,* says, it shall *never be forgiven, neither in this world nor in the*

the world to come, Matt. xii. 31, 32. O, Sir, keep your distance, drop no such hints here; *he that shall blaspheme against the Holy Ghost hath never forgiveness, but is in danger of eternal damnation;* because they said he hath an *unclean spirit,* Mark iii. 29, 30. and those that declare the *law of the Spirit of life leads* to licentiousness say little better; for they charge him with the *devil's works,* though they do not call him in express terms *an unclean spirit.* It is a bold, daring, presumptuous, perilous step; it is *spiritual wickedness* in the *worst sense;* it is leaving sin at the foot of a lawgiver that shed no blood; it is committing rebellion against HIM that *will* BY NO MEANS *clear the guilty,* Exodus xxxiv. 7. it is doing *despite* on the bounds of the most sacred enclosure; it is venturing on the most dangerous spot of *holy ground* in all the holy land. Sins against *God the Father* in *the law* are *pardoned*; he *that speaketh a word against the Son of man it shall be forgiven him;* but he that blasphemes against the Holy Ghost hath never forgiveness. He will by *no means* (no not by the *blood of Christ*) pardon those that are *guilty of the sin unto death,* 1 John v. 16. Let me as a friend remind you of, and recommend you to, David's prayer, *Keep back thy servant also from presumptuous sins, let them not have dominion over me; then shall I be upright, and I shall be innocent from the great transgression,* Psalm xix. 13.

F   I have

I have watched narrowly fo see what good effects this doctrine of yours produces among those where it is perpetually enforced, and I can see nothing produced to make me fall in love with it, unless it be blindness, confusion, feigned humility, and struggling under bondage; being influenced with malice against the gospel; calling every thing that tends to make poor sinners free and happy, Antinomianism, not knowing what they say, but taking it from their teachers. *The saints are a people that God has formed for himself to shew forth his praise*; he has *created them anew in Christ Jesus unto good works, which he hath before ordained, that we should walk in them.* It is therefore their new creation in Christ Jesus, and their abiding in him, *as the branch doth in the vine, that produces these good works* which they are to walk in. As they received Christ Jesus the Lord, so they are to walk in him. Every saint must acknowledge, as Paul did, that, *by the grace of God I am what I am.* If grace makes them what they are, sending them to the law will never mend this work, nor make the subjects of this workmanship better; *God's work is perfect, nothing can be added to it* by the the wisdom of men nor by the law of Moses; *the law made nothing perfect, but the bringing in of a better hope did* do it, Heb. vii. 19. The church is subject to Christ; subject to the civil power where they live, and subject to one another : but not

not subject to Moses, nor to his law, they *are no longer under a schoolmaster*, Gal. iii. 25. *no longer under tutors and governors*, Gal. iv. 2. they are not under the law but under grace. When the *false brethren* " came in to spy out the apostle's liberty, " that they might bring them into bondage, tell- " ing them that they must keep the law of Moses, " we gave place to them by subjection, no, not " for an hour (says Paul) ; nor did we reject the " truth and admit their yoke of bondage, no," we gave place not for an hour; that *the truth of the gospel might not continue with you*, Gal. ii. 4, 5.

My friend will be ready to say—the way to heaven is a difficult way to find ; and I answer it is so, because there is a *ditch* so close to it, which many fall into, being led by false preachers, deceitful workers, and blind guides, who turn from the *truth that came by Jesus Christ*, and get to groping about mount Sinai for help, till the old vail and the god of this world blind their eyes ; and when they have lost sight of the puzzling mystery of the gospel (for such it is to unconverted men) then they think they see every thing in the letter of the law and in themselves, and so become vain in their imaginations, their foolish hearts being darkened ; then they follow vain jangling, and make shipwreck of faith, lampoon the power of religion, become haters of those that are good, deceiving themselves and deceiving others, till they get desperate against the truth,

truth, and it becomes a vexation only to understand the report of the gospel, but the path of the just hath the light of God's countenance upon it: he that walks and lives by faith *is in the narrow way that leadeth unto life*, Matt. vii. 14. for the just man shall live by his faith, and he shall walk in newness of life. This is wisdom's way, a *path which no fowl knoweth, and which the vulture's eye hath not seen. The lion's whelps have not trodden it, nor the fierce lion passed by it*, Job xxviii. 7, 8. Christ is the way as well as the truth and the life; to live and walk by the faith of him is to walk safely indeed. *In this way of righteousness is life, and in the path-way thereof there is no death*, Prov. xii. 28. Though this way appears narrow and difficult, yet the poor believing sinner, who is nothing in himself, but looks to his Saviour for all, though he be *a fool he shall not err in this way:* the Lord has promised to guide him and uphold him; and I will, says God, *lead them in a way wherein they shall not stumble; for I am a father to Israel, and Ephraim is my first-born*, Jer. xxxi. 9.

The bad use that ungodly men may make of the truth of the Christian's liberty in the Spirit is not to silence spiritual ministers; Christ's yoke must be brought forth; the children of God must be fed; the gospel must be preached; the saints liberty must be shewed, and they cautioned not to abuse it, and counselled to stand fast in it;
notwithstanding

notwithstanding the villany of those that *come in privily to spy it out*. Ungodly men will abuse the most High God, and even the Bible itself; therefore no wonder if they abuse the sermons or writings of his servants. The impenitent infidel, whose mind and conscience both are defiled; to whom there is nothing clean; who are condemned already, and under the wrath of God; will turn every thing to bane. But are we to muzzle the truth, yoke the saints of God with Moses' law, and call the snares of death rules of life, to please them? No; this is putting *stumbling blocks before the eyes of the blind*, and making men *stumble at the law*, Mal. ii. 8. this is not declaring the whole counsel of God; this is not leaving the work with the Lord, who has power over all flesh, that he may give eternal life to as many as are ordained to it. We are not to make such men as these the objects of our fear in the pulpit, nor keep back God's word from his people on account of their abusing it: they called the *master himself Belzebub*; and what can be expected from such men but sin? *ministers are a favour of death unto death to them*, and are sent *to preach the gospel for a witness against them*; and their desperate wickedness against the gospel serves to shew us *that they were before of old ordained to this condemnation*, Jude 4.

I have considered the text you refer me to, " if ye love me keep my commandments," John xiv. 14.

and I find *his commandments are joyous not grievous*—for the commands are *that we should believe on him and love one another*. But those that call the law the believer's rule of life, and me an Antinomian, shew but very little of this love. He keeps the Saviour's commandments *who receives the word in an honest and good heart,* and keeps it; such receive the word with *power in the Holy Ghost, and in much assurance;* such and only such *keep the word of Christ's patience, and he will keep them from the hour of temptation,* Rev. iii. 10. He that keeps the Lord's commandments is united to him by the bond of love in the Spirit; *he that keepeth his commandment dwelleth in him and he in him;* he that is a stranger to this union is alive without the law— alive to sin and dead to God; for *hereby we know that he abideth in us, by the* quickening *Spirit which he hath given us,* 1 John iii. 24.

I have had a world of legal duties formerly pressed upon me, and I know what effect such preaching had; and I see it has the same in others that fear God. It serves to nurse the pride of those that know nothing of the power of godliness. I have heard misers, persecutors, and hypocrites, applaud and admire the doctrine, but they have been dreadfully exasperated at some who are called Antinomians, if they have happened to enforce the necessity of the Spirit's assistance in the performance of these things, and of their being done in faith.

Men

Men may load people as much as they please with moral, relative, and church duties; but if they spring not from union with the true vine; if not performed under the influence of the Spirit of God; if they are not done in faith, and with an eye to God's glory; they amount to nothing more than the works of the flesh, or *dead works*; while the legal performer is as proud as Satan himself; and, by resting in these things, is *farther from God's kingdom than publicans or harlots*.

A *devil transformed into an angel of light* is more dangerous than when he comes in character; that is, as an accuser, a thief, or a robber: nor does Satan do the seeking sinner so much hurt *when he throws him down and rents him*, Mark ix. 20. as he does when he points us to legal preachers, or *ministers of the letter*, crying out these men are the *servants of the Most High God, that shew unto us the way of salvation*, Acts xvi. 17. He was as much a *devil* when he promised this world and the glory of it to Christ as he was when he wished him to *throw himself from the pinnacle of the temple*, Luke iv. 9. Satan sometimes turns reformer in times of danger, when the gospel makes a stir in his territories, then is the time that he fires the zeal and increases the numbers of moral preachers; he knows what the law can do—if that had never appeared in the world, the devil had never got one human soul into hell: *the law worketh wrath; for where no law is, there is no transgression,* Rom. iv. 15. consequently no transgressors. He knows that the *strength of sin is the law,* 1 Cor. xv. 56. better than we do; and he knows that those who are *under the law of death are under the law of sin;* hence it is that he never stirs men up to reproach, revile, belie, scandalize, or persecute, a graceless preacher of moral duties; for it is by the instrumentality of such men that he has brought thousands to his dark dominions: by such preachers as these the devil keeps both the pulpit and the pew—he stirs up the preacher to blind the people, and the people to applaud their blind guide; and thus the God of this world holds both the leader and the led. When he stirred up the Jewish priests to reject Christ, and cast out his disciples, he became head ranger both of the temple and the synagogue. The doctrine that routs the devil is preaching the kingdom of God, which consists in righteousness, peace, and joy in the Holy Ghost; telling Zion that her King is come. When the disciples preached this the Saviour saw *Satan like lightning fall from heaven,* Luke x. 18. he cast abroad the rage of his wrath and set the world in a blaze. This sort of preachers are the only adversaries that the devil has got, he gains ground by the others. He was very nigh bringing over the whole *church of Galatia* by the instrumentality of moral preachers. If God does not *uphold his people with his free Spirit,* Psal. li. 12.

I much

I much queftion if any other yoke will do when trials come on; for my part, I never found any doctrine that would beget fouls to God, keep them alive, make their minds heavenly, their converfation pure, keep their confciences tender, or make their lives exemplary, but that of enforcing regeneration, or a fpiritual birth; juftification by faith; union and fellowfhip with Chrift by love; and a walk in the teftimony and liberty of the Holy Ghoft. However, this I can fay—that the religion that God has taught me has been fufficient to make me induftrious and willing to live honeftly; and I muft declare, and will with my dying breath, that I never knew what happinefs, peace, reft, quietude, comfort, joy, or pleafure, meant until Jefus Chrift appeared to my foul: in him I have feen the perfection of all beauty; I have felt him to be the foundation of all real happinefs: the light of his countenance, and the anticipation of his love, is the quinteffence of all that is called pleafure; and to have him is to be poffeffed with an immortal, incorruptible, undefiled, and neverfading inheritance; which has fo crucified me to this world, and to the pleafures of it, that I have juft as much defire to return to it again as Abraham had to return to Err of the Chaldees, when God had promifed to be his fhield and everlafting reward in the land of Canaan.

Whatever

Whatever the law of God *enforces* the Spirit of God *impresses* the mind with, and leaves the impression as legible *upon the fleshly tables of the believer's heart, as ever he did on the two tables of stone,* 2 Cor. iii. 3. The devil is never more to be suspected than when he appears in a pulpit in a large wig and long bands, with a grave countenance, an audible voice, ambiguous speech, zeal mixed with candour, enforcing moral virtue, and bringing in Christ as an example, but not as the *root of the matter;* nor yet enforcing the need of his Spirit, nor of union with him. These things, and a few zealous strokes at the power of religion, under the name of enthusiasm, and a candid application to those blind and bond children, that cannot see through their mask, have been of very great use to the devil, because it has served to stumble the faithful and establish the Pharisee. Such as these have sent my soul bleeding home many a time swaddled with the spirit of bondage; sin has took an occasion by the commandment until the corruption of my heart and my carnal enmity has been stirred up against God, my mind begloomed with horror, and terrors have drove to my feet; wrath has seemed to pursue me; Christ and comfort was gone; my sins, that had been long pardoned, came afresh to my remembrance; my heart was filled with hard thoughts of the Saviour, and the devil tempting me; that Christ had

left

left me, was become my enemy, and, as a proof of it, he was now purfuing me with fire and fword. But when the Lord appeared and delivered me, I then faw the bondage was from the law, not from the Saviour, and that it was the devil purfued me, not the Lord: I could fee the difference between the tempter and my great Deliverer. And all this was communicated to my foul from the pulpit, and that by the devil himfelf in a large wig and a long band. Chrift calls the fcribes, notwithftanding their long robes, a *generation of vipers*; and fays they were *of their father the devil and his works they did*, in binding *grievous burdens on men's fhoulders, which they never touched*, though others' laboured hard under them. If Satan can get preachers to obfcure the gofpel and enforce the law, he knows the old vail will gather on the minds of the people; and when a man is blinded you may lead him any where; and he fhall never know the want of a leader while Satan can furnifh the world with blind guides: for it is by thefe men that he leads them into the ditch. Such preaching drives many poor diftreffed fouls from all religion; they hear of nothing but wrath and duty: and the more they labour the worfe they get, and then they fhake off all, and are glad to get out fo; and fuch become the greateft enemies to religion afterwards: and the inftruments of all this mifchief are legal preachers—for *without Chrift man can do nothing,*

nothing, John xv. 5. it is looking to Jesus that enlightens us; abiding in the cleft of the rock that shelters us from Satan's rage. Souls flying here are compared to doves flying to their windows, where they are sure of light; but going to the law *is going to blackness, and darkness, and tempest, and to the burning fire,* Heb. xii. 18. which pursues the sinner. Satan is not displeased at men's dressing up the law, calling it the believer's rule of life, the law of love, the law of kindness, &c. He knows the law is the *snares of death,* that has entangled all the prey which that artful fowler has caught. This law is the sinner's *adversary* that entangles him in his sin, *and delivers him to the judge; and the just judge delivers him by the law to the tormentor,* Matt. xviii. 34. Are there souls in hell?—it was the law that cast them, condemned them, and fixed them there. Are they holden with the *cords of their sin?*—the *strength of those cords is the law,* 1 Cor. xv. 56. Are they under the curse?—*then they are under the law,* Gal. iii. 10. Are they under the dominion of eternal death?—they received it from the law, which is the *ministration of death,* 2 Cor. iii 7. Are their souls boiling with desperate indignation against God?—the motions of sin are by the law. Are they under the wrath of God? *the law worketh that wrath,* Rom. iv. 15. Are they in *utter darkness?*—it came from the law, *which is blackness and darkness,* Heb. xii. 18. Are they in *hell-fire?*—they received it *from the fiery law,*

law, Deut. xxxiii. 2. Can they never come out of the bottomless pit?—the immutable sentence of the law is the *gulf fixed;* let the law be repealed, and nothing can detain the prisoner : but *not a jot or tittle of that law can fail,* therefore no jail-delivery can ever take place; *what God doth, it is done for ever.* The devil has not a greater friend in this world than a blind legal preacher ; nor the children of God a greater enemy. I have sorely felt the effects of such a ministry ; and I know where such ministers are better than they do themselves. Those that are spiritual, says Paul, *judge all things, but themselves are judged of no man,* 1 Cor. ii. 15.

If the covenant of grace does not afford the believer a rule of life, it must be very deficient ; however, Paul could bring a rule from thence sufficient for the believer to live by, walk by, worship by, and converse by. God's sovereign will is man's rule ; and to the saints *God makes known the mystery of his will according to his good pleasure,* Eph. i. 9. which runs thus—*This is the will of him that sent me, that every one which seeth the Son, and believeth on him, may have everlasting life : and I will raise him up at the last day,* John vi. 40. This mystery is called, by way of distinction from the law, God's GOODWILL *towards men, which brings peace upon earth, and glory to God in the highest,* Luke ii. 14. it is the *goodwill of him that dwelt in the bush,* Deut. xxxiii. 16. when this is revealed to men's hearts

hearts by the Holy Ghost it is called *the mystery of faith in a pure conscience*, 1 Tim. iii. 9. and this is the saints all-sufficient rule;—by faith the just man is to live; by faith, and not by sight, is the just man to walk; in the Spirit, not in the letter, is the just man to serve; in spirit and in truth is the just man to worship: he that is faithful unto death shall have the crown of life; the end of faith is the *salvation of the soul*. Let the law be what it may, and aim at what it pleaseth, the *end of the commandment is charity out of a pure heart, of a good conscience, and of faith unfeigned*, 1 Tim. i. 5. he that swerves from this turns aside to vain jangling; knows not what he says, nor whereof he affirms, 1 Tim. i. 6. God tells us *to hold faith and a good conscience, which some having put away, concerning faith have made shipwreck*, 1 Tim. i. 19. Let men bring what rules they please from the law; let them drive their flocks with that storm as much as they can; I know the real believer, though he be not to *make haste*, in one sense, will hasten his *escape from that stormy wind and tempest*, for he knows that whatsoever is not a *fruit of the Spirit* is a work of the flesh; whatsoever service be performed, if not done under the influence of the Spirit of life, it is a *dead work*; and if not done in faith it is sin; for *whatsoever is not of faith is sin*—for without *faith it is impossible to please God*. We read of ministers of the Spirit and of ministers of the letter; and if there be

any

any such things as ministers, and a ministration of the Spirit, I think these things belong to that ministration, and to preach them is doing the work of an evangelist, and making full proof of the gospel ministry.

No man ever heard me say or hint a syllable against the *goodness of the law*; the law is good, *and it works death in us by that which is good*, Rom. vii. 13. I suppose no nation hath more wholesome laws than this; and I believe no nation under heaven of its size sends more criminals out of the world by a halter. There are heathen nations destitute of such wholesome laws that do not execute half the number of felons that we do. Be so kind, Sir, as to send me word what the law requires that this better testament does not furnish a believer with; when the imperfection or deficiency of this *law of the Spirit* is made to appear, we shall be able to justify the conduct of those who send numbers that have begun in the Spirit to the law to be made perfect by the flesh. This must be done, or else we shall conclude that this doctrine, of allowing the believer no rule of life but the law, is no better, in the language of the Holy Ghost, than witchcraft. *O, foolish Galatians, who hath* BEWITCHED *you, that you should not obey the truth! This only would I learn of you, Received ye the Spirit by the works of the law, or by the hearing of faith? Are ye so foolish—having begun in the Spirit,*

are

are ye now made perfect by the flesh? Gal. iii. 1, 2, 3. these people did not intend to give up the Saviour, they were only going to help him; they did not intend to cast off the Spirit, they were only going to perfect that which was *lacking* in his work; they had begun in the Spirit, and were going to the law to be made perfect. Ah! says Paul, the law belongs to the children of the flesh; to them it speaks; the works of it are the works of the flesh. Your perfection from thence will be only perfection in the flesh, and where you go for perfection there you must go for righteousness. Christ is our *righteousness and sanctification too*—go to the law for one, and you must go the law also for the other; by going for perfection there that yoke will entangle you again, and bring you into bondage. God makes us perfect by the Spirit, which unites to and makes us one with Christ, in *whom we are complete.* These poor souls were going to be circumcised, and take the law on them as a rule of life, in order to perfect the Spirit's work. These preachers, Paul says, bewitched them, zealously affected them; yea, they would have excluded them from Christ, that they might affect them: ye are *fallen from grace,* says Paul, *Christ shall profit you nothing.*

Peter on the mount of transfiguration did not intend to exclude the Saviour when he said —*Let us build three tabernacles; one for thee, one for Moses, and one for Elias*; which when Moses and Elias heard, they

they withdrew, as all good servants ought to do. *And there came a voice out of the cloud, saying, This is my beloved Son, hear him.* Moses refigned his office to the Mediator of the better testament, who is the end of the law for righteousness, to whom Moses had borne witness. And Elias withdrew also, and left the Saviour in his prophetic office, as that great prophet to whom all the prophets gave witness; and I believe that Jesus is (in the highest sense) that Elias that was for to come. And it is said that, suddenly, when the disciples had looked round about, that is, after Moses and Elias, *they saw no man any more save Jesus only with themselves*, Mark ix. 4, 5, 6. 8. and he is sufficient; and it is a thousand pities that we have so many in our days who are fetching Moses in again; but they will get neither peace nor good works from him, but rather confusion. The master and the servant must not be coupled together; they are not co-masters, co-rulers, co-yokers, co-mediators, co-builders, co-lawgivers, co-husbands, nor co-sovereigns. The *law was given by Moses, but grace and truth came by Jesus Christ.* There are several of our present divines who, notwithstanding their zeal for Moses, and desire to copy after him, do not at all imitate him in this point; he kept the blessing of Abraham and the curse of the bond-woman apart; he pointed out two different mountains for the blessing and the curse; and different men were

named

named and appointed for each work; these were typical of *ministers of the Spirit*, and those *of the letter; Simeon, Levi, Judah, Issachar, Joseph, and Benjamin, shall stand on mount Gerizim to bless; and Reuben, Gad, Asher, Zebulun, Dan, and Naphtali, shall stand on mount Abel to curse,* Deut. xxvii. 12. 13. Zion and Sinai must be kept apart; they are two different mountains, and two different cities are founded on them; *for this Agar is mount Sinai in Arabia, and answereth to* JERUSALEM *which now is, and is in bondage with her children,* Gal. iv. 25. and wo be to that man that is found a citizen of this bond city in the great day! *Tyre, Nineveh, Babylon* the literal, and *Babylon the mystical*, may one day understand the awful allegory, when they will be found to belong to *the city of destruction,* Isa. xix. 18.

But God hath built his city on the mountain of eternal election, he hath laid his everlasting foundation there, *his foundation is in that holy mountain, and he loveth the gates of Zion more than all the dwellings of Jacob,* Psalm xxxvii. 2. God hath founded this city himself, and the poor of his people shall trust in it, Isaiah xiv. 32. *He hath appointed salvation to be her walls and bulwarks;* he is known in her palaces for a refuge; his dwelling-place is in Zion; *he hath chosen her, she is to be his rest for ever: here will he dwell; for he has desired it. He will abundantly bless her provision and satisfy her poor with bread; he will clothe her priests with salvation, and her saints*

saints shall shout aloud for joy, Psal. cxxxii. 13, 14, 15. It was this city that Abraham and Isaac had in view; they kept it in the eye of their faith, and it made them *forget their own country and their native home*; *they sought a city that hath foundations, whose maker and builder is God,* Heb. xi. 10. Upon *mount Zion God hath commanded the blessing, even life for evermore,* cxxxiii. 3. To this mountain Jacob looked when he was on his death-bed, and knew that God's eternal love was the bounds of this city, and that all his blessings came from thence. *The blessings of thy father have prevailed above the blessings of my progenitors, even to the utmost bound of the everlasting hills,* Gen. xlix. 26. This is Solomon's *little city with few men in it, which the great king came to besiege with great bulwarks, which the poor wise man by his wisdom delivered, who is so little regarded for his great deliverance,* Eccl. ix. 14, 15, 16. This is the only *city of refuge* under the gospel; and *it is near to flee into, and it is a little one*; but God will never *destroy it,* nor the *lot of his inheritance* who become *citizens* of it.

In vain men grope in the wilderness to find it, and all religion is vain that doth not bring men to it—*The labour of the foolish wearieth every one of them, because he knoweth not how to go to the city,* Eccl. x. 15. It is on the *holy hill of Zion that God has set his king*; and the *daughters of Zion are to go forth and behold their King Solomon, whom Zion their mother*

mother crowned in the day of his espousals, and in the day of the gladness of his heart, Song iii. 11. This is the *city of the great King*, of which *such glorious things are spoken*; it is *beautiful for situation*, being built upon the Rock of ages; encompassed with a *mountain of brass*, Zech. vi. 1. A *city set on a hill that can never be hid*, Matt. v. 14. and is the *joy of the whole earth*; for *God is known in her palaces for a refuge*, Psalm xlvi. 3. he hath redeemed her with judgment, and her converts with righteousness; and *out of Zion the perfection of beauty God hath shined*, Psalm l. 2. It is his own metropolitan; *it is the city of the great King*: this *mountain brings peace to the people, and the little hills* (obtain it by faith in an imputed) *righteousness*, Psalm lxxii. 3. *The river of life, and all its streams of comfort, are to make glad this city of God*, Psalm xlvi. 4. divine singers and all celestial musicians *shall be there*; *all God's springs* of love, mercy, and peace *are in her*, Psalm lxxxvii. 7. and every saint of God, whether a native of *Rahab, Babylon, Tyre*, or *Ethiopia, shall be born in her*; *this and that man shall be born there*, Psal. lxxxvii. 4, 5, 6. As soon as *Zion travels she brings forth*, and *of her womb shall a nation be born at once:* of the *breasts of her consolations* shall every babe of grace *suck*, and *upon her knees* shall every child of God be *dandled*; for God hath *extended peace to her like a river, and righteousness as an overflowing stream.*

Zion's

Zion's laws are in the heart of Zion's King; the *law of faith*, the *perfect law of liberty*, and the *law of the Spirit of life*, go forth from hence: *out of Zion shall go forth the law, and the word of the Lord from Jerusalem*, Isaiah ii. 3. And as for them that say, *Let us break their bonds asunder, and cast their cords from us*—he that dwells in heaven shall laugh, and have them in derision. The throne of grace is in Zion—*whosoever shall call on the name of the Lord shall be delivered; for in mount Zion shall be deliverance, as the Lord hath said, and in the remnant whom the Lord shall call*, Joel ii. 32. This is *our* comfort, that God will never depart from this city; *for the name of the city from that day shall be, the Lord is there*, Ezek. xlvii. 35. from this city *God sends help to his people*; they are strengthened *out of Zion*: and it is against this city that all our blind legal watchmen are levelling their *vain janglings*; but *all that fight against mount Zion and her munition, and all that distress her, shall be as the dream of a night vision*, Isaiah xxix. 7. The Highest himself shall establish her; *God shall help her, and that right early!* she shall *never be moved*; not *one of her stakes shall ever be removed*, nor any of her cords ever be broken, Isaiah xxxiii. 20. This *city shall be let down out of heaven at the final conflagration, and shall be at the right hand of the King when he makes all things new,* Rev. xxi. 2. 5. and all that *compass about this beloved city fire shall come down from God out of heaven and*

and devour them, Rev. xx. 9. To *mount Zion, the city of the living God, the heavenly Jerusalem, are all the saints to be brought* ; here are the *innumerable company of angels :* this is the *general assembly and church of the first-born, which are written in heaven*; here is *God the judge of all,* and here are *the spirits of just men made perfect*; here is *Jesus, the mediator of the new covenant, and the blood of sprinkling, that speaketh better things than that of Abel*; and what would the believer have more ? *See that ye refuse not him that speaketh*, Heb. xii. 22, 23, 24, 25. It is *out of Zion the Deliverer shall come* to the Jews when he appears *to turn away ungodliness from Jacob,* Rom. xi. 26. Blessed are those *ambassadors* who stick *by this city,* especially when she is as she is now, LOW *in a* LOW PLACE : *blessed are they that sow beside all waters, that send forth thither the feet of the ox and the ass*, Isaiah xxxii. 19, 20. O Zion, if my pocket did but spring as fast as my heart, I could write a volume upon thee; thou art almost hid by the smoke of Sinai : surely those that despise thee know not the thoughts of the Lord ; and those that depart from thee shall never divide the spoil. They never could enjoy the freedom and privileges of this city ; they never could be within her walls ; they were only spies that came to count her towers, observe her palaces, and mark her bulwarks; and are hastening away, having robbed her ambassadors of the name EVANGELIST, which belongs to Zion's watchmen and no others;

and can be no more applicable to a *minister of the letter* than the word *grace* would be to one of the *dukes of Edom.* However, God calls them in his word by other names; such as *vain janglers, subverters* of his people, *tempters* of God, *bewitchers* of his saints, *authors of shipwreck, zealous affecters* but not well, *excluders* from Christ, *perverters* of truth, *spies* that come in to see the liberty of his children, and bring them into bondage; *tinkling cymbals*; and declares *that if an angel from heaven preach any other gospel than that which his servant Paul preached, let him be accursed,* Gal. i. 9.

As to the secret lashes that these gentlemen have given me, is little grief to me; I know that God the Saviour revealed this doctrine to my soul, and I defy either *hill* or *dale, scot* or *lot, parsons* or *parson-makers, groves* or *avenues, wilks* or *mussels, wills* or *testaments,* kinsmen or uncles, *towers* or *castles, backs* or *bellies, knights* or days, *watts* or whims, to prove that God's word points out either LAW or RULE that mount Zion doth not furnish the believer with. Zion's *King sends the rod of his strength from hence, his kingdom stands not in word but in power, in righteousness, peace, and joy in the Holy Ghost; for he that in these things serveth Christ is acceptable to God, and approved of men,* Rom. xiv. 17. 18.

No man can couple these two mounts together; and he that is a stranger to the sentence and wrath of the one is a stranger to the feasts and joys of the other; such never publish their conversion, nor their

their call to the miniftry; and it is beft not, for any difcerning Chriftian may eafily perceive that they are ftrangers to both. I doubt not but men may learn fome of thefe things notionally, and preach them; but what know they of thefe things? What know they of the terrors of God, the law of faith, the law of the Spirit of life, of the dominion of grace, union with Chrift, and liberty by the Spirit? To plunder and preach thefe things without an experience of them in the heart, is only a *parable in the mouth of fools.* I did not fo learn thefe things, nor did I find them in any authors; for the few that I have read, whether they were called Antinomians, or whether they were minifters of the letter, which now a-days are called evangelifts, neither of them pleafed nor inftructed me; for thofe called Antinomians feemed to have no experience, and thofe who pretended to be evangelifts feemed to have as little underftanding: this I know, that while I fuffered the terrors of Sinai I was diftracted, and when I was brought to Zion I was clothed and in my right mind. I did intend to have fent out a Riddle at the end of this; but, as it fwells too big for the pockets of many of my friends, muft poftpone that till another opportunity.

F I N I S.

Juft Publifhed, by the fame Author,

The Way and the Fare of a Wayfairing Man.

www.ingramcontent.com/pod-product-compliance
Lightning Source LLC
Chambersburg PA
CBHW020153170426
43199CB00010B/1021